NEGATIVE CAMPAIGNING

An Analysis of U.S. Senate Elections

RICHARD R. LAU
and
GERALD M. POMPER

Newspaper account
1992–2002

ROWMAN & LITTLEFIELD PUBLISHERS, INC.
Lanham • Boulder • New York • Toronto • Oxford

MD

2004

ROWMAN & LITTLEFIELD PUBLISHERS, INC.

Published in the United States of America
by Rowman & Littlefield Publishers, Inc.
A wholly owned subsidiary of The Rowman & Littlefield Publishing Group, Inc.
4501 Forbes Boulevard, Suite 200, Lanham, MD 20706
www.rowmanlittlefield.com

P.O. Box 317, Oxford OX2 9RU, UK

British Library Cataloguing in Publication Information Available

Library of Congress Cataloging-in-Publication Data

Lau, Richard R.
    Negative campaigning : an analysis of U.S. Senate elections / Richard R.
Lau and Gerald M. Pomper.
        p.   cm.—(Campaigning American style)
    Includes bibliographical references and index.
    ISBN 0-7425-2731-X (cloth : alk. paper)—
    ISBN 0-7425-2732-8 (pbk. : alk. paper)
    1. Political campaigns—United States.   2. United States. Congress.
Senate—Elections.   I. Pomper, Gerald M.   II. Title.   III. Series.
JK2281.L38   2004
324.7'0973—dc22   2004002086

Printed in the United States of America

∞ ™ The paper used in this publication meets the minimum requirements of
American National Standard for Information Sciences—Permanence of Paper for
Printed Library Materials, ANSI/NISO Z39.48-1992.

CONTENTS

TABLES AND FIGURES

Tables

Figures

ACKNOWLEDGMENTS

W E ARE PLEASED to record our considerable debts. We have benefited greatly from collaboration with our students and colleagues. Earlier versions of this research were presented at professional political science meetings where our papers were coauthored by Erlinda Mazeika and Grace Mumoli. Mazeika, Mumoli, and Sameeha Hussein coded most of the newspaper articles about the Senate campaigns, and students in Lau's research methods classes also canvassed Senate campaigns from 1998 and 2002. More recently, Tim LaPira provided great help in coding variables on campaign effects. We appreciate the help of the following individuals: Charles Franklin for sharing his data about the 1988 and 1990 Senate election campaigns, used in earlier versions of this research, and here providing lagged values of campaign tone, vital instruments in some of the 2SLS analyses; John Brehm, Alan Gerber, and Jerry Hagstrum for sharing various other information; and Stanley Feldman and Mark Kamlet for statistical advice.

We gratefully acknowledge the courtesy of editors—particularly Greg Caldeira, David Farrell, Ada Finifter, and David Lowery—and publishers in allowing us to reprint sections of the following articles that originally presented the research of this book:

"The Effects of Negative Political Advertisements: A Meta-Analytic Assessment," *American Political Science Review* 93 (December 1999): 851–875.

"Negative Campaigning by U.S. Senate Candidates," *Party Politics* 7 (January 2001): 69–87.

"Effects of Negative Campaigning on Turnout in U.S. Senate Elections, 1988–1998," *Journal of Politics* 63 (August 2001): 804–819.

"Effectiveness of Negative Campaigning in U.S. Senate Elections," *American Journal of Political Science* 46 (January 2002): 47–66.

We owe past readers of these papers a brief explanation: What they will see in this book differs from what they have read previously. Chapter 2 is essentially reproduced as originally published. It was coauthored by Lee Sigelman, George Washington University; Caroline Heldman, now at Whittier College; and Paul Babbitt, now at Southern Arkansas University. We appreciate their contributions and also thank Karen Hartman for locating relevant studies and Allen Wilhite for helpful comments on the original paper.

The data on which the analysis of U.S. Senate elections is based have changed substantially, however. Most obviously, we dropped the 1988 and 1990 election years from our study and added data from the two most recent (2000 and 2002) biennial Senate elections. Thus roughly one third of the data being analyzed in this book is new. This keeps the number of election years (six) and number of Senate elections available for study about equal, but it removes the awkwardness of relying on two different data sets, collected and coded by two different research teams, for the crucial data about the nature of the Senate campaigns. In our earlier work we utilized campaign data from 1988 and 1990 that was originally gathered by Charles Franklin of the University of Wisconsin. Although there will inevitably be slight differences in how he and we coded the data, the biggest difference between the two data gathering efforts is that he subscribed to the largest newspaper in each state holding a Senate election and relied entirely on these newspapers for his estimates of the nature of the campaign, while we sampled articles from online databases, primarily Lexis/Nexis. Lexis/Nexis contains both large and small newspapers but may not include the largest newspaper in a state. It is unclear what, if any, bias this difference introduced to our earlier analyses, but it is certainly better to have a consistent source of data for our primary variable of interest.

This change also allowed us to employ Franklin's data as *lagged* indicators of campaign tone from previous Senate elections for the earliest elections in our sample, which was a crucial instrumental variable for our two-stage least squares analysis. As it turns out, this change substantially improves the predictive power of that instrument, and thus improves our first-stage estimates of campaign tone.

We also took this opportunity to try to improve the measurement of the campaigns that *we* had originally coded for the Senate elections between 1992 and 1998, focusing on races with relatively few newspaper articles, and thus relatively noisy estimates. We first searched through Lexis/Nexis again to see if any new newspapers had been added to the database; we were able to find a few more articles in this manner. Then we turned to the Dow Jones database and searched anew, limiting our data collection to newspapers that are not included in Lexis/Nexis. (These two large newspaper databases share a goodly number of newspapers in common, but they each contain some newspapers that the other does not.) Our extended search located an additional 109 newspaper articles about Senate elections between 1992 and 1998, articles that were not a part of our earlier data coding. This allowed us to include two additional states from the earlier period in our analysis and to substantially improve our estimates of the nature of the campaign in nine others. It also allowed us to double our minimum standard for number of codable statements from the candidates for inclusion of a campaign in the study.

Finally, we relied on data in the various *Almanac of American Politics* volumes (e.g., Barone and Ujifusa 1999), which in turn relied on estimates from the Census Bureau, for measures of the percentage of various demographic groups living in each state. Of course, the 1992 and 2002 *Almanac*s report the actual counts (or more accurately, the much better estimates) of these data from the 1990 and 2000 censuses. Judging from the data in the 2002 *Almanac*, many of the census estimates from the previous years were deficient. We therefore assumed a linear change between 1990 and 2000, and "corrected" our state-level demographic figures for the 1992 to 1998 election years. We assumed a constant rate of change to project figures for 2002.

Over the years, we have gained much from discussions with friends and colleagues on this research. In particular, we learned from Larry Bartels, John Geer, Jane Junn, Stanley Kelley, David Redlawsk, Stephen Salmore, and Daniel Tichenor. As with all of this volume, we thank panel participants and anonymous reviewers for very helpful comments. Marlene M. Pomper made important contributions by reading manuscripts and page proofs. Karen Hartman and Marlene M. Pomper gave us substantial emotional support by cheering on our work.

This research has been aided by academic generosity. Lau conducted much of this research as a fellow at the Center for the Study of Democratic Politics at Princeton University. Rutgers University provided research grants for Pomper, and the Eagleton Institute of Politics provided space, financial aid, and the considerable secretarial talents of Joanne Pfeiffer. In achieving publication, we have gained much from Jennifer Knerr and Renee Legatt of Rowman and Littlefield, and appreciate the expert copyediting of Jenn Nemec and Patricia MacDonald.

Our greatest debts are to our families, who provided us with joy when we were with them, and forbearance when we were not. This book is another reflection of our love.

The Problem of Negative Campaigning

ELECTION ARDOR was at fever height. The incumbent candidate was denounced as the head of the "monarchical party in the United States," intent on excluding from office "*honest Americans*, who braved the perils of a long and bloody war." His challenger would allegedly trample those morals that "guard the chastity of our wives and daughters from seduction and violence . . . and shield our religion from contempt and profanation" (Cunningham 1972, 54–56).

Foreshadowing many contemporary campaigns, this nasty battle came in 1800, the first contested presidential election in the United States. Featuring two patron saints of the nation, John Adams and Thomas Jefferson, it also marked the onset of negative campaigning in American politics. The practice would continue from the founding of the republic to the present. Even the most revered presidents were never safe from allegations and slurs: Andrew Jackson for his war record, Abraham Lincoln for his black parentage, Franklin Roosevelt for his disability, Bill Clinton for adultery, George W. Bush for alcoholism. Reviewing "the fine art of president-baiting," Meg Greenfield concluded, "Any nation that has survived the ministrations of . . . such crooks, frauds, murderers, traitors and half-breeds as our Presidents have been has reason to be proud of itself" (Greenfield 1964, 29).

Negative campaigning has been evident in other races as well, often validating Lord Bryce's ([1888] 1995, Vol. 1, 879) characterization of American electioneering as "a tempest of invective and calumny . . . thick with charges, defences, recriminations, till the voter knows not what to believe." By the time of the presidential primaries of 2004, negative campaigning had itself become a focus of candidates and the press (Halbfinger 2004).

In U.S. Senate elections, the practice abounded as recently as 2002. In New Jersey, incumbent Democrat Robert Torricelli came under attack for accepting illegal gifts from a Korean favor-seeker. He retaliated by publicizing his opponent's decade-old opinion that highway checkpoints for drunken driving were "a gross violation of proper governmental boundaries" (Kocieniewski 2002). In Montana, a Republican challenger all but withdrew from the contest when Democratic ads implied that he was gay (Anez 2002). In Georgia, Democratic senator Max Cleland, a quadriplegic Vietnam veteran, was defeated for reelection when his concerns about homeland security legislation were portrayed as unpatriotic. (See Jalonick 2002 for an account of this and other Senate races in 2002.)

If not new, negative campaigning does seem more prevalent today. To judge from the unprecedented loud volume of complaints registered in recent years about the negativism of campaigns, matters have only deteriorated in contemporary politics. In the late 1970s and early 1980s, when political action committees targeted a number of congressional incumbents for attack, negative campaigning entered the current high-intensity phase of the "emotional sine wave" it has ridden over the course of American history (Gronbeck 1994, 61).[1]

What are the consequences of this barrage of negativism? Public discussion of negative political campaigning has been dominated by two responses to this question—one short-term and pragmatic, the other long-term and normatively despairing.

First, both practitioners of negative campaigning and its harshest critics believe that it works. Campaign strategists portray negative advertising as a potent political force, citing dramatic instances in which attack ads have been instrumental in turning a campaign around, such as Cleland's upset defeat in the 2002 Senate race and George H. W. Bush's come-from-behind victory over Michael Dukakis in 1988. Republican pollster Richard Wirthlin (1987, 3) contends that "a negative attack can take a virtual unknown against an apparently strong incumbent and provide a tremendous and strong margin"; Democratic consultant Philip Friedman agrees: "The big question in most campaigns . . . is whose negative campaign is better. If it's negative, it works. If it's positive, save it for your tombstone" (Henneberger 1994, 45).[2]

The impact of negativism is commonly attributed to television's increasing dominance of modern political campaigns. Television, it is said, has "granted the manufacturers of campaign discourse some Svengalian powers that print and radio lacked" (Jamieson 1992, 9). In the pre-television era, the mass media were thought to have minimal political effects, largely reinforcing existing attitudes and commitments (e.g., Berelson, Lazarsfeld, and McPhee 1954; Lazarsfeld, Berelson, and Gaudet 1948), but television apparently has changed all that.

When skillfully used, television's multiple modes of communication and powerful ability to orient attention can invite strong, unthinking negative responses in low-involvement viewers. By overloading our information-processing capacity with rapidly paced information, televised political ads can short-circuit the normal defenses that more educated, more highly involved viewers ordinarily marshal against suspect claims (Jamieson 1992, 50).

Recognizing the medium's ability to transmit their messages dramatically, rapidly, and widely, candidates for high office have increasingly built their campaign strategies around television in general and television advertising in particular. But the high cost of television advertising means candidates want to make sure they get their money's worth, and that evidently translates into more and more negativism. As political scientist Herbert Alexander put it, "The high cost of television means now that you have to go for the jugular," a tendency that leads Alexander to predict "even more negativity than we've experienced now" (Purdum 1998, 4).

The second, and more serious, danger of negative campaigning is its perceived corrosive influence on participatory democracy, as "the electronic equivalent of the plague" (West 1993, 51). Democracy is a dialogue between putative leaders and citizens. Campaigns provide the most obvious and the loudest forums for this dialogue. Candidates try to persuade voters to cast ballots and to support their causes. Voters respond by coming to the polls and selecting their preferred candidates. The quality of the dialogue can wane, however, if candidates speak poorly or if voters close their ears. The asserted increase in negative campaigning leads, observers fear, to a concomitant decrease in the civic worth of political campaigns.

Beset by the unseemly spectacle of candidates doing "whatever it takes" to win (as George H. W. Bush vowed in 1992), citizens are repulsed. As one political consultant has observed, "In a campaign of negative ads fighting negative ads, what incentive is there for the viewer to go to the polls? Obviously, both these candidates are turkeys. The potential voter is left with a disgruntled sentiment that it's a shame someone has to win" (Laczniak and Caywood 1987, 21).

"Campaign discourse is failing the body politic in the United States," writes a leading analyst (Jamieson 1992, 11), expressing a widely shared concern. Negative politics, critics fear, could undermine the American political system—with obvious and serious consequences for democratic politics generally. Negative campaigning has been associated with a decrease in voter turnout (Ansolabehere, Iyengar, Simon, and Valentino 1994; Goldstein 1997a), an increase in political cynicism (Thorson, Ognianova, Coyle, and Denton 1996), a decrease in political efficacy (Ansolabehere and Iyengar 1995; Thorson et al. 1996), and a decrease in "public mood" (Rahn and Hirshorn 1999; Thorson et al. 1996). Such systemic effects are certainly consistent with a commonsense psychology of citizen reaction to widespread negative campaigning.

And yet conventional wisdom is not always right. If we systematically examine the evidence in the existing research literature, the inordinate power of negative political campaigning to persuade is—at best—unproven (see Finkel and Geer 1998 for a recent example; see the following chapter for a comprehensive review). In 1995, there were but ten publications on negative campaigning's effectiveness, none involving representative population samples. Only three of these studies reported effects of any magnitude, and of these, two were counter to the intentions of the candidate who sponsored the negative advertisements. One would have to conclude from the available evidence that the effectiveness of negative campaigning is at best a research hypothesis, and quite possibly a myth. Still, there is sufficient concern to justify fuller examination of the subject. That is our purpose in this book.

Studying Negative Political Campaigns: What, Who, When

We focus our studies in three respects. (1) We carefully define negative campaigning. (2) We deal only with elections to the U.S. Senate. (3) We include all competitive elections to that body from 1992 to 2002. The remainder of this chapter explains these specifications. Details of the data and methods can be found in appendix B.

Negative Campaigning

Because "observers often define negativity as anything they do not like about campaigns" (West 1993, 46), we must carefully distinguish between the directional meaning of negative—statements in opposition to a person or program—and the evaluative meaning—statements that are "unfair" because they are (subjectively) disliked or distrusted. Although often confused, the two are not necessarily linked. A positive campaign still might be unfair (e.g., an appeal to whites to support racial discrimination). A negative campaign still might be fair (e.g., documented criticism of an opponent's corruption in office). Candidates can lie (or more generously, stretch the truth) about their opponents in negative campaigning, but they can do the same about themselves in what we call positive campaigning. The motivation is the same either way, and it is unclear why distortion would be any more likely in one form than the other.[3]

In this book we restrict our meaning to direction, the simple and reasonably objective criterion. Negative campaigning is talking about the opponent—criticizing his or her programs, accomplishments, qualifications, and so on. Positive campaigning is just the opposite: talking about one's own programs, accomplishments, qualifications, and so on. In most of the analysis, we will combine statements on both the issue positions and the personal qualifications of the candidates, but we will distinguish these modes at some points.

In recent discussions of televised political advertising (Bartels et al. 1998; Jamieson and Waldman 1997; Jamieson, Waldman, and Sherr 1998), a more elaborate distinction has been drawn between "advocacy," "comparative," and "attack" political advertisements. In addition, the argument is made that negative advertising is too often conflated with unfair advertising, while attack advertising is a less affectively loaded term; thus researchers are urged to replace the terms *positive* and *negative* with *advocacy* and *attack*. We are not convinced these new terms are any less affectively loaded but will none-theless try to employ them when we are talking about political *advertising*.

Our chief dependent variable involves the political *campaign* more broadly, however, and for this purpose we find the tripartite categorization less useful. While individual political advertisements may be entirely advocacy or entirely attack, all campaigns are inherently comparative. There are degrees of difference, of course: Some candidates focus primarily on themselves and their own accomplishments and proposals in their campaigning, while others focus primarily on the asserted shortcomings of their opponents. This is the variation we hope to capture and explain. But the comparative category would be too broad, almost all-inclusive, if applied to campaigns rather than to advertisements. To be more precise, and avoid any arbitrary cutoffs, we employ a single positive–negative continuum and seek to learn the overall direction, or tone, of these comparisons.

The Senate

Most of the American literature on political campaigns focuses on presiden-tial elections. From a research perspective, however, presidential campaigns are poor venues for exploring campaign effects. Of all political figures, incum-bent presidents and their high-profile challengers are the most well-known figures, and both major-party candidates are well financed. As a result, these candidates are unlikely to be "redefined" by obviously partisan attacks from their opponents or overwhelmed by their spending.

Furthermore, media coverage of presidential elections tends to be objec-tive and evenly balanced between the contestants, making it less likely that one candidate will be disadvantaged in the press (although a candidate may be hurt by the "frames" used in the media; see Jamieson and Waldman 2002). The presidential campaign also gets so much free coverage from the national media—coverage that candidates can only partially influence—that candidate-sponsored advertisements, speeches, and rallies comprise only a small proportion of the total information available about the competitors.

As an alternative, we believe that statewide elections provide a much more promising opportunity for exploring campaign effects (see Franklin 1991 for similar arguments). On the one hand, statewide races are prominent enough to attract, and thus require, substantial campaign funds. There are real cam-paigns to study. But on the other hand, statewide candidates tend to be less well known than presidential candidates, and these races get little coverage in the national media and substantially less coverage than the presidential cam-paign even in the local media. As a result, the respective campaigns can influ-ence more of the readily available information about the candidates.

Senate elections particularly provide some of the most prominent exam-ples of negative campaigns. The 2002 races mentioned earlier are illustrative but by no means isolated events. In earlier years, U.S. Senate campaign advertisements were replete with Jerry Springer–style vitriol, with critical commentary present in 71 percent of advertisements aired in the final week, according to one account (Sack 1998). The New York senatorial campaign, for instance, centered on characterizations of incumbent Republican Alphonse D'Amato as a lying opponent of children's education, and of Democratic congressman Charles Schumer as a derelict advocate of tax increases. Readers can surely provide other egregious examples from many prior elections in different states.

Of late there has been an upsurge of research on Senate elections (e.g., Abramowitz 1988; Campbell and Summers 1990; Carsey and Wright 1998; Franklin 1991; Gerber 1998; Kahn and Kenney 1999b; Westyle 1991). Although incumbents typically win reelection, many face stiff electoral challenges. Indeed, when incumbent senators sought reelection over the past three decades (i.e., from 1970 through 1998), they were defeated about 19 percent of the time. Thus the outcome of many Senate campaigns is not a foregone conclusion.

Senate elections, furthermore, are methodologically superior for scholarly analysis. Most obviously, far more cases exist: There are sixty-seven elections for senators for every quadrennial presidential contest, providing a considerable contrast to the usual paucity of systematic evidence about what candidates actually *do* during campaigns.

Research on Senate elections allows us to incorporate a wide variety of electoral influences, both national and local. National factors include the popularity of the incumbent president and the state of the national economy. Among local factors, an acknowledged influence is the "quality" of the candidate challenging an incumbent (Squire 1992). Money is certainly important, and campaign spending figures are readily available. We can examine the different effects of spending and other campaign influences in races by incumbents, challengers, and open-seat contestants and also compare the conventional view that money matters much more to challengers (Abramowitz 1988; Jacobson 1978) with a more current dissenting view (Gerber 1998; Green and Krasno 1988). We will also be able to disentangle the causal links between spending and election outcomes. We include the most important factors from prior research in our own analyses.

The Times

We limited our study of Senate elections to the past decade, 1992 to 2002. During this period, there were six national elections. In each, as provided in the Constitution, one-third of the hundred seats were filled, as well as some additional seats that became vacant through deaths and resignations (eight over this period). These six election years therefore comprised two complete cycles of Senate races. All but five of the individual Senate contests were competitive between the two major parties, at least nominally. They also covered a variety of political circumstances—three elections in off years and three elections with a presidential race on the ballot. The results also varied, as specified in table 1.1. Democrats won two and Republicans one of the presidential contests; in the Senate, Republicans gained seats in three of the elections, Democrats made gains in one year, and two were standoffs.

We have much information available for analysis. We invite our readers to follow us as we explore this rich political world. Six chapters follow. We will first review the previous literature on negative advertising (chapter 2). Our substantive studies examine the extent of negative campaigning (chapter 3) and then analyze its actual effects on election results (chapters 4 and 5) and on voter participation and attitudes toward the political system (chapter 6). A full listing of previous research and of our methods and data can be found, respectively, in appendix A and appendix B. After these empirical studies, we will discuss the normative merits and deficiencies of negative campaigning and suggest improvements in the electoral process to facilitate voter choice (chapter 7).

Table 1.1   Winners in U.S. Senate Races, 1992–2002

	1992	1994	1996	1998	2000	2002	Totals
Democrats							
Incumbents	14	14	7	14	9	10	68
Hold Open Seats	5	0	5	1	3	1	15
Challengers	1	0	1	2	6	1	11
Take Open Seats	1	1	0	1	1	0	4
Republicans							
Incumbents	10	10	12	12	12	14	70
Hold Open Seats	3	3	6	1	1	5	19
Challengers	2	3	0	1	1	2	9
Take Open Seats	0	5	3	2	1	1	12
Net Change	0	+7R	+2R	0	+5D	+2R	+6R
Totals (D/R)	21/15	15/21	13/21	18/16	19/15	12/22	98/110

Note: Democrat Ron Wyden won the special election in Oregon in early 1995 to replace Republican Senator Bob Packwood. This outcome is included in the 1994 column above, but this out-of-cycle election is excluded from all subsequent analyses.

Notes

1. How sharp this rise has been is a matter of some dispute, as can be seen by comparing the trend lines estimated by Jamieson, Waldman, and Sherr (1998); Kaid and Johnston (1991); and West (1993). In point of fact, little hard evidence supports the prevalence of negative political advertising before 1996.

2. Perloff and Kinsey's (1992) survey of political consultants makes it clear that these opinions are well in keeping with the consensus among these campaign specialists.

3. It is unclear whether, in practice, claims made about an opponent during a political campaign are generally less truthful than claims made about oneself. But in principle, by definition, this cannot be assumed. In fact, Jamieson, Waldman, and Sherr (1998) report that at the presidential level at least, attack (negative) advertisements are more truthful than advocacy (positive) advertisements.

The Literature of Negative Campaigning

O UR RESEARCH ON negative campaigning is informed by previous scholarship. In this chapter we survey this research as it stood at the end of the 1990s. Using the technique of meta-analysis, we find this previous work to be inadequate in demonstrating the impact of negative campaigning. In the rest of this book, we seek to repair these deficiencies.

We examine the claims that negative political advertising is a potent political force, simultaneously shaping election outcomes and causing citizens to tune out and turn off from the political process. In theory—that is, in both social psychological (Lau 1985) and rational choice theory (Riker 1996; Skaperdas and Grofman 1995)—negative advertising *should* work, and there clearly is no shortage of dramatic examples and expert testimony that it *does* work. Even so, the most sophisticated research to date on political advertising is only partially consistent with these two ideas. In a series of carefully controlled laboratory experiments, for example, Ansolabehere and Iyengar (1995; see also Ansolabehere et al. 1994) uncovered surprisingly little evidence that campaign ads shape voters' choices between opposing candidates. However, these experimental studies, buttressed by analyses of state-by-state voter turnout patterns in the 1992 Senate elections, did bear out the charge that negative advertising turns many citizens away from politics, leading to a significant dropoff in voter turnout.

Why not, then, consider these matters settled? Why not accept the argument that negative ads undermine public support for and participation in the electoral process? One reason for skepticism is that both practitioners and critics dwell on instances in which negative advertising is thought to have been decisive, but they tend to ignore counter examples. The failed presidential campaigns of George Bush in 1992 and Bob Dole in 1996, Michael Huffington's losing Senate bid in 1994, and Al Checchi's and Jon Christensen's abortive gubernatorial races in 1998 serve as reminders that attackers do not always win.[1] Moreover, no single research study should be treated as definitive. Tellingly, reinterpretations of Ansolabehere and Iyengar's findings have appeared (Bartels 1996), as have new studies (analyzed later in the chapter) reporting contrary findings.

Political consultants and pundits should not be taken at their word when they testify to the potency of negative advertising. What, then, is the appropriate response? The usual scholarly answer would be to propose yet another round of empirical studies, and well-designed new research on negative political advertising would certainly be welcome. We would argue, however, that the highest immediate priority is to sift carefully through the available evidence to see what can be learned from data already at hand. In recent years a substantial body of research has accumulated on political advertising in general and negative political advertising in particular. What do these studies, taken as a whole, reveal? Does the preponderance of evidence bear out the claims about negative advertising that have so often been made and seem to be so widely accepted?

This question is not just of passing interest to casual observers of the American political scene. For those who believe that "politics matters"—that it makes a difference whether a Democrat or a Republican sits in the White House or in the governor's mansion, or which party controls Congress— knowing whether a common campaign tactic works is important. In the heat of an election campaign, long-term qualms about the erosive impact of negative ads on participatory democracy may well give way to the immediate goal of winning an election. In the long run, however, the charge that the increased negativism of campaigns is undermining the American political system cannot be taken lightly. Does anyone doubt that the stability of the American system of government itself might be threatened if turnout continues to fall and if cynicism toward those in office continues to rise? These are vital questions for political science—and for American democracy.

These are also questions that political scientists *should* be able to answer. A criticism often leveled against the social sciences is that research findings do not accumulate. One set of researchers addresses a certain question with a particular methodology, another group of researchers addresses the same question with a different methodology, a third set of researchers addresses a related question with yet another methodology, and none reach a definitive conclusion.

Realistically, though, no one study can ever provide all the answers to any worthwhile scientific question, and no one method is superior in every situation. Science progresses when multiple researchers employ different research techniques to explore a research question. There comes a time when we must take stock of what has been learned. But no comprehensive, systematic attempt has been made to review research on negative political advertising, to reconcile or even document contradictory findings, or to determine where the bulk of the evidence lies.[2]

To provide such a review, we have conducted a meta-analysis, an undertaking common in some fields but still rare in political science. This technique involves the statistical integration of research findings, usually from separate studies conducted independently of one another.[3] In a meta-analysis the findings themselves are treated as primary data, the goal being to establish the consistency and magnitude of the relationships in question. This is a complicated process, which we attempt to explain in detail in appendix B; some readers may want to leave these intricate details unread.

The basic conclusion of this chapter severely challenges conventional wisdom. After examining 117 pertinent findings in fifty-two different studies (listed at the end of the book as appendix A), we find that statements about the effectiveness of negative campaigning, and about its deleterious effects on the broader political system, are unproven at best and often just wrong. Through the new research of this book, we seek more informed and more accurate judgments.

What Does Negative Advertising Really Do? And Not Do?

We present these results in three sections, based on thirteen possible outcomes. We begin with a test of (1) affect toward the negative ads themselves, whether people actually dislike this form of political communication. Six measures assess the intended consequences of negative political ads: (2) affect for the target of an ad; (3) affect for the sponsor of an ad; (4) differential affect for the target and the sponsor; (5) intention to vote for the target or the sponsor; (6) actual vote for the target or the sponsor; and (7) memory of the ad. A successful negative ad should reduce affect for the target (the opponent of the ad's sponsor); not reduce affect for the sponsor, or at least increase affect for the sponsor relative to the target; enhance the likelihood of voting for the sponsor rather than the target; and convey a memorable message.[4]

Six additional measures assess the unintended consequences of negative ads: (8) intention to vote; (9) actual vote turnout; (10) trust in government; (11) political efficacy; (12) knowledge about the candidates running in an election; and (13) public mood. These potential effects are not directly related to a voter's choice between the sponsor and the target; they gauge the systemic effects of negative political advertisements—their impact on voter turnout, trust in government, and the like.

The effect of negative advertising, if any, is shown by a statistic we call "effect size," which measures the difference between people who have or have not been exposed to negative advertising. Statistics are calculated for each of the thirteen possible outcomes and presented in tables 2.1 and 2.2. Table 2.1 is a simpler presentation that conveys the basic results. Table 2.2 is a more elaborate analysis, including the effect size, but its results are essentially similar.

Affect toward Negative Political Ads

If there is one point on which virtually everyone seems to agree, it is that no one really likes negative political ads.[5] The data analyzed here do not speak

Table 2.1   Summary of Uncorrected Parametric Results

Dependent Variable	Number of Findings	Mean	Median	Range	Standard Error
Affect for Ad Itself[a]	10	−.44	−.34	−3.12 to 1.01	.35
Intended Effects					
Memory for Ad[b]	14	.34	.17	−1.15 to 3.86	.32
Affect for Target[c]	16	.38*	.34	−.48 to 1.90	.16
Affect for Sponsor[d]	25	−.51**	−.35	−2.05 to .75	.13
Differential Affect[e]	4	−.87	.10	−4.38 to .72	1.19
Vote Intention[f]	13	−.06	.00	−2.40 to 1.77	.29
Actual Vote[g]	5	−.24	−.17	−.58 to −.06	.09
Unintended Effects					
Intended Turnout[h]	4	−.04	−.05	−.18 to .12	.07
Actual Turnout[i]	15	−.06	.02	−1.39 to .49	.11
Other Systemic Effects[j]	11	−.21	−.08	−1.45 to .14	.13

*$p < .05$ **$p < .01$

[a] The studies in table 2.1 are numbered consecutively. Data relevant to affect for the ad itself come from studies 14, 15, 24, 35, 37, 40, 42, 44, 48, and 49.

[b] Data on memory for ads come from studies 4, 5, 15, 22, 23, 24, 25, 27, 32, 33, 39, 42, 43, and 44.

[c] Data on affect for the target of negative ads come from studies 4, 6, 13, 14, 20, 21, 24, 27, 29, 32, 35, 36, 40, 42, 43, and 52.

[d] Data on affect for the sponsor of negative ads come from studies 4, 6, 13, 14, 15, 16, 17 (two data points), 20, 22, 24, 27, 29, 30, 32, 34, 35, 36, 40, 41, 42, 43, 44, 49, and 52.

[e] Data on differential affect come from studies 10, 26, 47, and 52.

[f] Data on vote intention come from studies 1 (two data points), 6, 20, 22, 24, 30, 34, 36, 40, 41, 42, and 44.

[g] Data on actual vote come from studies 7, 26 (two data points), 46, and 51.

[h] Data on intended turnout come from studies 1, 22, 31, and 37.

[i] Data on actual turnout come from studies 2, 8 (two data points), 9, 10, 11 (two data points), 12 (two data points), 19, 26, 28, 31, 45, and 50.

[j] Includes two analyses of public mood (studies 38 and 45), four of political efficacy (studies 1, 9, 12, and 45), two of trust in government (studies 29 and 45), and three of knowledge about the candidates running in an election (studies 3, 18, and 45).

directly to this point, for findings concerning evaluations of negative ads were not coded against an absolute "neutral" point. However, these data do enable us to assess the closely related claim that negative ads are liked less than positive ads.

If affect is markedly lower, on average, for negative than for positive ads, then the average size of the ten pertinent effects should be well below zero as we have coded the data; that is, subtracting affect for positive ads from affect for negative ads should produce a negative effect size estimate. However, evidence for the oft-asserted abhorrence of negative political ads turns out to be surprisingly weak. When the combined significance approach is followed, the null hypothesis that no significant effect exists can be rejected ($z = -9.43$, $p < .001$), but this is due almost entirely to one extremely significant result. When we take a parametric approach (as shown in table 2.1), even allowing for this one extreme negative value (−3.12), the mean uncorrected

Table 2.2 Summary of Corrected Parametric Results

	Number of Studies	Total # Subjects	Corrected for Sampling Error		Corrected for Attenuation due to Measurement Error		Corrected for Sampling Error, Measurement Error, and Variation in Strength of IV	
			Effect Size	Standard Error	Effect Size	Standard Error	Effect Size	Standard Error
Affect for Ad Itself	10	1,580	−.52	.44	−.61	.51	−.63	.63
Intended Effects								
Memory for Ad	14	7,529	.88	.69	1.11	.79	.55	.49
Candidate-Centered Intended Effects	35	14,458	−.14	.09	−.16	.11	−.15	.12
Unintended Effects								
Combined	22	45,948	.05*	.02	.07**	.05	.04	.05
Just Turnout	17	44,644	.03	.07	.04	.08	.02	.09

*$p < .05$ **$p < .01$
Note: This analysis aggregates across multiple findings (within category) reported by any study. IV represents independent variable.

effect size for these ten outcome measures is only −.44. This signifies an average difference of only about four-tenths of a standard deviation between affect for positive and negative political ads. This is in the direction that would be expected based on the frequent expressions of disgust with negative ads. However, the variability of the ten effect sizes sounds a caution against interpreting this difference as consistent with expectations. More formally, the standard error is nearly as large as the mean effect size itself, and the 95 percent confidence interval for the unadjusted mean effect size extends well into positive territory (−1.23 to +.35). Thus, considered as a body of evidence bearing on the issue of affect for negative ads, the research literature provides no reliable statistical basis for concluding that negative ads are liked less than positive ones.

The more elaborate analysis adjusts for sampling error, measurement unreliability, and variation in treatment strength (shown in table 2.2). With these adjustments, the mean effect size increases to −.63, but the standard error also rises, to +.63. For the adjusted means, the 95 percent confidence interval runs all the way from −2.06 to +.80. For neither the unadjusted nor the adjusted effects, then, can we safely reject the null hypothesis of no difference between affect toward negative and positive political ads. It may be that most people do not like campaign ads very much, but whether a political advertisement is positive or negative seems not to be the crucial factor. Or it may be that the widespread hand-wringing about negative ads is largely ritualistic or is focused on a few negative ads that are seen as excessive rather than on negative ads as a genre. If anything, this initial result should be encouraging to those who employ negative ads despite the "fact" that people dislike them. According to the evidence that we have located, this "fact" is considerably overstated.

Intended Consequences: The Effectiveness of Negative Political Ads

If negative political advertising works, it should have positive consequences for its sponsors and negative consequences for its targets. More specifically, negative messages should be more memorable than positive ones; they should cause affect for the opponent to decline; they should, at the very least, not greatly deflate affect for the sponsor; they should have a net positive effect on evaluations of the sponsor relative to those of the opponent; and, most important, they should increase the probability of voting for the sponsor rather than the opponent.

The evidence detailed in appendix A does not bear out these suppositions. Most of the effect sizes fall very close to the zero point, and about as many are below as above zero. In fact, under the nonparametric combined significance test, the null hypothesis that the hypothesized effect is not found in any of the populations studied cannot be rejected ($z = -1.10$, $p > .20$)—and the bulk of the findings are in the direction opposite of what the sponsors of these ads intend. Of the findings for the specific dependent variables in this category in table 2.1, the only two with mean positive effect sizes (i.e., the only two that run in the hypothesized direction) are memory for the ad and affect for the target of the ad, and only the latter is statistically significant. That is, it does appear that the sponsoring candidate's opponent is liked less when he or she is attacked by political advertising. Even so, this intended effect is counterbalanced by an even stronger and highly significant decrease in liking of (i.e., a "backlash" against) the sponsor—an effect that sponsors of such ads certainly do not want to achieve.

We collapsed the multiple indicators of intended effects into two broad categories before adjustments: findings about the ad itself (i.e., memorability), which are presumably a secondary consideration for those who run the ads, and findings about the candidates (the rest of the findings in this group).[6] The mean unadjusted effect size is $-.28$, counter to what the sponsor of an ad would want. When the estimates are adjusted for sampling and measurement error and variation in treatment strength (table 2.2), the mean candidate-centered effect shrinks somewhat but is still negative, albeit not statistically significant; a zero effect is easily encompassed by the 95 percent confidence interval, which ranges from $-.39$ to $+.09$. The average corrected effect size for memory of the ads rises as high as 1.11, but the standard error rises commensurately, and this moderately high mean effect is still not different from zero, with the 95 percent confidence interval ranging from $-.51$ to $+1.61$. In sum, across these multiple criteria, *there is simply no evidence in the extant research literature that negative political advertisements are any more effective than positive political ads.*

Unintended Consequences: Do Negative Ads Damage the Political System?

Finally, we turn to the claim that negative political ads lead citizens to tune out and turn off from politics in general and from campaigns in particular. If this is true, then the effect sizes for the "unintended consequences" outcome measures should be well below zero, as we have coded the data; that is, the unintended consequences of negative ads should be more in a negative direction than those of positive ads.

Of the findings included in the meta-analysis, thirty bear on this claim. For the nonparametric combined significance approach, the null hypothesis of no significant effect in any of the populations studied cannot quite be rejected with a one-tailed significance test, which is appropriate here ($z = -1.07$, $p < .07$). The sample sizes of the thirty data points tend to be very large, however, so it is not surprising that some of them are significant. More telling is the pattern of results: fifteen are negative, including five significant results, but fourteen are positive, including two significant findings. When these findings are adjusted for sampling error, unreliability of measurement, and treatment strength in table 2.2, the mean effect size is slightly greater than zero. The story does not change if we limit the analysis to studies of intended and actual turnout.[7] In sum, *we uncovered little evidence to warrant the fears of those who believe that electoral participation is imperiled by the increasingly widespread use of negative political advertisements.* Participatory democracy may be on the wane in the United States, but the evidence reviewed here suggests that negative political advertising bears relatively little responsibility for such trends.

Further Analyses

Scientific research is always tentative, subject to error, and subject to change with better evidence. It may be that the conclusions we have reached thus far hide some flawed techniques or need to be qualified. Through further and somewhat esoteric analysis, we now consider three potential problems that, if present, could undermine the results reported to this point.

First, might these results have been unduly influenced by a few findings based on atypically large samples? This seems most likely for the "unintended consequences" findings, a few of which involve an extremely large number of cases. To probe this possibility, we first counterfactually assumed that the three studies with extremely large sample sizes (Finkel and Geer 1998: $N = 12,252$; Geer and Lau 1998: $N = 8,069$; Kahn and Kenney 1998: $N = 6,110$), which together accounted for almost 58 percent of the total cases in this category, had "only" half of their actual total of 26,431 cases. This caused the adjusted means reported in table 2.2 to decrease slightly, but they remained positive. Then we reduced their sample sizes even further, by a factor of five, and halved the recorded sample sizes in the other six studies with more than 1,000 cases. This reduced the adjusted means slightly more, but they remained above zero, and it left our conclusions essentially unchanged. Thus our results seem fairly insensitive to extreme values, for the estimated effect size remained small even when we "fixed" the large-sample problem.

Second, how might our conclusions change if findings that have escaped our notice were taken into account? There is a bias toward statistical significance in published studies. To cope with this problem, Rosenthal (1979) devised a technique for estimating how many extra findings with effect sizes averaging zero would have to be located to reduce an observed significant mean effect size to nonsignificance (see also Hunter and Schmidt 1990; Orwin 1983). Here we face the opposite problem. Having uncovered mostly nonsignificant mean effects for the "intended consequences" measures in particular, we are concerned that large-effect findings may exist without having made their way into the research literature. It is conceivable, for example, that some political consultants possess such evidence but have not published it or presented it publicly.

To pursue this possibility, we reversed Rosenthal's logic by calculating how many such findings would have to exist to convince us to alter our conclusions. In light of the observed range of effect sizes for "intended consequences" outcome measures, we would classify an effect size of $+1.00$ as very strong—stronger, in fact, than any we actually observed. Assuming that the newly available effect sizes averaged $+1.00$ and were based on the same average number of cases, measurement reliabilities, and combined variances as the findings considered here, at $\alpha = .05$ it would take *twenty-five of them*, not counterbalanced by any contrary new evidence, to increase the mean unadjusted effect size significantly above zero. Given the general bias toward significance in published research, it seems much more reasonable to assume that additional *small*-effect findings exist that so far have escaped our notice than to assume that we have missed so many sizable effects. All in all, then, it would take a mass of very strong and entirely uncontradicted new evidence to lead us to conclude that negative political ads work. Because the possibility that such evidence exists seems remote, we place considerable confidence in our conclusion that negative political ads fall significantly short of achieving their intended results.[8]

Third, might stronger effects emerge if we disaggregated the data? In aggregating findings across studies, have we ignored crucial differences among studies that, if taken into account, would bring stronger effects to the surface? The best context for addressing this issue is provided by findings on the intended consequences of negative ads, for which there are enough findings to allow testing of some subsidiary hypotheses.

We considered several possibilities:

1. Perhaps, to follow up on a point raised earlier, the definition of "negative ad" matters, such that entirely negative ads are no more effective than entirely positive ads, but comparative or contrast ads are most effective. From a rhetorical point of view, a case has been made that comparative or contrast ads are optimal for effective electoral decision making (Jamieson, Waldman, and Sherr 1998). Empirically, however, it makes no difference whether entirely negative or more comparative political ads are contrasted with positive ads: $t(38) = -.73$, ns.

2. Perhaps design quality has increased over time, in which case more recent studies should be more likely to have reported, correctly, that negative ads are more effective.

3. Alternatively, it is possible that, just as military leaders often rely on outdated strategies because they worked so well in the last war, nega-

tive ads, though once effective, have become so commonplace that they have lost their effectiveness (Lau 1985). In that case, there should be a negative correlation between time and effect size. However, contrary to this idea as well as the previous supposition, the correlation between year of publication and effect size ($r = -.11$) does not differ from zero.

4. Perhaps experiments, because they tend to be artificial, produce unrealistic results, while survey-based studies produce the expected results. However, a t-test contrasting the effect sizes of findings based on experiments versus survey-based findings revealed no significant differences: $t(36) = 1.07$, ns.

5. Perhaps actual ads and/or ads featuring real candidates are more likely to be effective than ads created solely for research purposes. However, the observed differences were small ($ts < 1$) and ran in the wrong direction.

6. Perhaps studies that either manipulated or directly coded the contents of political ads are better indicators of the true strength of negative ads, compared with studies where the negativism of the ads is inferred from secondary (e.g., newspaper) accounts. However, the observed differences were small in magnitude [$t(38) = .57$, ns] and ran counter to this hypothesis.

7. Perhaps findings from studies based on student samples are idiosyncratic, while studies utilizing adult subjects and representative samples produce the expected results. However, the use of student samples did not significantly affect the effect size: $F(3,36) = .77$, ns.

8. Perhaps televised negative ads work better than their printed counterparts. However, studies using video ads as stimuli produced no greater effects than studies presenting ads through other media: $t(38) = -.80$, ns.

9. Perhaps researchers in certain disciplines are more sensitive to the context of a campaign, and thus more likely to uncover the predicted positive effects. However, a one-way analysis of variance contrasting studies published in the fields of communications, political science, and psychology uncovered no such differences: $F(2,37) = .05$, ns.

10. Perhaps better designed studies are more likely to produce the expected results. However, there was no significant difference in effects between studies we subjectively categorized as of higher quality and those we considered of lesser quality: $F(2,37) = 1.47$, ns.

11. Perhaps exposing subjects to a larger number of ads produces greater effects. However, there was no correlation between effect size and the number of ads to which subjects were exposed: $r = .09$, ns.[9]

Having considered and rejected all these possibilities, we conclude that if there is some critical factor that must be present for the expected effects of negative advertising to emerge, we have not been able to identify it.

Implications

Our synthesis of findings reported in the research literature has not borne out the main claims that have been made about the effects of negative advertising. The great majority of the effects that have been reported are of modest magnitude, with effect sizes clustered in a narrow band extending from slightly above zero to slightly below zero. We observed no significant tendency for negative ads to evoke lower affect than other campaign ads, contrary to the oft-voiced contention that citizens reserve special disdain for negative ads.

This result does not mean that negative political ads are well liked. Indeed, there is abundant evidence that they are not; for example, 75 percent of those interviewed in a 1994 poll said they were turned off by negative ads (Brack 1994). Rather, it simply means that, according to the available evidence, negative political ads are not disliked significantly more than other political ads—or, for that matter, than ads in general. In an era when majorities or substantial minorities of adult Americans consider television advertising unhelpful, unbelievable, and misleading, and respond by leaving the room, attending to chores, or channel-surfing during commercial breaks (Mittal 1994), should the unpopularity of negative political ads be considered especially noteworthy?

Nor, more importantly, did we uncover consistent, let alone strong, evidence that negative ads work to the advantage of their sponsors and/or the disadvantage of their targets. In this respect, it would appear, à la Newton's third law, that for every research finding about the effectiveness of negative advertising, there is an equal and opposite research finding. Only a handful of the positive effect sizes we catalogued are large, and these are counterbalanced or even overbalanced by another handful of effect sizes on the negative side. There simply is no compelling evidence that negative advertising works.

Of course, the effects of negative campaign ads need not be statistically significant in order to be politically significant or even decisive. Even a tiny advantage to the sponsor could be enough to determine the outcome of a close election, and even an attack that fails to sway voters could cause the target to divert precious resources in rebuttal. The results of our meta-analysis should not, then, be interpreted as saying that negative advertising is invariably a poor tactic. However, in general, negative campaign ads appear to be no more effective than positive campaign ads—if anything, somewhat less so. Thus, while we concede that a well-conceived negative advertising campaign could be a key to electoral success, the same can be said, and with somewhat greater confidence, about a well-conceived positive advertising campaign.

Finally, our meta-analysis also failed to confirm the widely held view that negative advertising should bear a major share of the blame for the widespread political disaffection of recent decades. The effects we observed for the "unintended consequences" measures are too small in magnitude and too mixed in direction to provide empirical warrant for heated claims that negative ads are undermining public confidence and participation in the electoral process. We should note, however, that all the studies analyzed here have focused on the immediate or short-term effects of viewing negative ads rather than on the long-term consequences of being subjected to a continuing barrage of such ads in election after election.

A quarter of a century ago, McCombs and Shaw (1972) attributed the prevailing lack of understanding of the impact of political advertising to the dearth of research on the subject. Since then, a great deal of research has been completed. But if the findings reported here are valid, widespread misunderstandings remain, at least in the form of overly expansive claims about the effects of negative ads.

Why are claims about the effectiveness of negative advertising so far removed from the findings reported in the research literature?[10] Part of the answer is undoubtedly that until the publication of Ansolabehere and Iyengar's *Going Negative* in 1995, academic research findings hardly dented the consciousness of those shaping public discourse concerning negative advertising. Nor are campaigners, consultants, and pundits immune to a wide array of perceptual and attributional biases (see, e.g., Kahneman, Slovic, and Tversky 1982; Fiske and Taylor 1991). Three such biases may be noted:

1. In campaigns in which both sides go on the attack, the well-known tendency toward internal attributions of success and external attributions of failure could lead winners to credit their own "brilliant campaign strategy" and losers to blame their opponents' "vicious attacks." Both of these claims would bolster the impression that negative advertising works, even though it obviously did not work for the losers.

2. A different bias that would produce the same result is the tendency to overgeneralize a vivid example that is easily retrieved from memory. For instance, a reasonably well-informed American, if asked to name a presidential campaign in which negative advertising was especially prominent, might well mention the 1988 race, with its images of revolving prison doors, a filthy Boston harbor, and Michael Dukakis riding awkwardly in a tank. Of course, in the following two presidential campaigns, the main attacker (Bush in 1992, Dole in 1996) lost, but it is the vivid exception—1988, when Bush's attack ads "worked"—that would probably spring to mind, forging an illusory correlation between going negative and winning.

3. More broadly, people often misperceive, reinterpret, or ignore information that is inconsistent with their preconceptions; any or all of these tendencies could lead candidates, consultants, journalists, and

political reformers to exaggerate the effectiveness of negative political advertising.

Which, if any, of these explanations is most accurate must remain a matter for speculation at this point. What should not be seen as speculative is the conclusion that prevailing understandings of the effects of negative political ads need fundamental rethinking—a process already heralded by the recent spate of research on negative political advertising. Contrary to ideas that are currently widely accepted, the extant research literature provides no significant support for the suppositions that negative political ads are especially disliked, are especially effective, or substantially undermine public support for and participation in the electoral process.

The Need for More Research

Examining the scholarly literature, we were struck by the dearth of solid research on some of these questions, particularly the effectiveness of negative campaigning, the very basis for its widespread popularity. Before we started our research there were only three extant studies of the effectiveness of negative campaigning where the dependent variable was an actual election outcome, and all were at the aggregate level of analysis.

Part of the reason for the lack of good solid research on the effects and effectiveness of negative campaigns is the methodological difficulties of documenting *any* kind of campaign effects. Consider for a moment just a few of those difficulties. On one side of the campaign contest is a candidate who has probably spent much of his adult life gaining the experience and skills to run for higher political office and win the party's nomination to run for an office such as senator. The candidate has the contacts or personal fortune to raise several million dollars to spend on this campaign, and he can afford to hire the best media consultants and pollsters, who will do everything they can with the candidate's money to get the citizens of the state to vote their way. But on the other side is an equally qualified and well-financed candidate from the other party running for the same office, who can also afford to hire very skillful consultants to run her campaign, who will do everything they can to get the citizens of the state to vote *their* way. We could have two very skillful campaigns; each alone would easily have persuaded the voters of a state to support its candidate. Run simultaneously, however, they precisely offset each other. And, of course, two ineffective and unpersuasive campaigns would result in the same outcome. How then can we, as researchers, tell the difference?

Moreover, we have good reason to expect that *any* political campaign, no matter how skillfully designed and well financed, will have only very limited success in achieving its goals because most citizens, most of the time, pay very little attention to politics. Keeping food on the table, the bills paid, the lawn cut, and the children happy, healthy, and doing well in school is more than enough to fill most people's days well into the evening, leaving relatively little time for relaxation, personal growth, or fulfilling one's citizen duty by paying attention to politics. For most people, politics are too removed from their daily lives, too difficult to fully understand, and too inconsequential to be worth the effort. Instead, citizens (i.e., those who even bother to go to the polls) rely on various cognitive shortcuts or heuristics that are largely independent of the current campaign to help them decide how to vote. Thus a third and very real possibility is that the nature of the political campaigns themselves is largely irrelevant to the outcome of the election because so few people are paying attention to the campaigns.

We do not attempt to provide a complete list of all the methodological difficulties of detecting media effects of any type, and our readers should rest assured that we have come nowhere near exhausting the list. Nor have we begun to address any of the techniques that researchers have developed to overcome those difficulties—techniques that we will describe (and illustrate) throughout the remainder of this book. Our point here is to remind readers of the enormity of the goal we have set for ourselves. There are very good reasons for the dearth of solid research in this area!

Nonetheless, we seek to test the effects and effectiveness of negative campaigns more fully. We develop what is by far the largest and most comprehensive data set on the nature of political campaigns that any researchers have ever used. We go beyond advertising and look at the broader range of campaign tactics, and we will employ an extensive array of statistical techniques to help overcome methodological hurdles. These data and techniques are described and explained in detail in appendix B. Equipped with these resources, we are prepared to reach grounded conclusions on the extent of negative campaigning, its effects on election outcomes, and its possible dangers for the American democratic process. We now turn to this substantive analysis.

Notes

This chapter is based on Richard R. Lau, Lee Sigelman, Caroline Heldman, and Paul Babbitt, "The Effects of Negative Political Advertisements: A Meta-Analytic Assessment," *American Political Science Review* 93 (December 1999): 851–875.

1. Nor, in principle, *can* attackers always win. When two opponents attack each other, as occurred in the North v. Robb Senate race in 1994 and the Torricelli v. Zimmer Senate race in New Jersey in 1996, only one can succeed (Lau, Pomper, and Mumoli 1998, 2).

2. Lin (1996) provides a descriptive overview of research on negative political advertising, and Hale (1998) presents a meta-analysis of a small subset of the studies reviewed here.

3. Standard sources on meta-analysis include Cooper and Hedges (1994); Glass, McGaw, and Smith (1981); and Hunter and Schmidt (1990).

4. However, for a critique of recall as an indicator of the effectiveness of an ad, see Haskins (1964).

5. The idea that voters profit from hard-hitting presentations of the differences between candidates does have its defenders (e.g., Mayer 1996). It is not the sheer existence but the seeming ubiquity of negativism and the excesses to which it is often carried that excite the greatest criticism.

6. Most studies in this literature report multiple findings that are relevant to the meta-analysis. When those findings fell into distinct categories, we treated them separately. When multiple findings involving the same set of subjects were in a single category, however (as is the case for the candidate-centered intended consequences), we averaged across the multiple effect sizes that were based on the same set of subjects to come up with a single effect per data set. Occasionally a study reports multiple relevant findings from distinct sources or data sets (e.g., Ansolabehere and Iyengar 1995), and in such cases we retained the distinct findings. Thus the sixty-three individual candidate-centered effects summarized in table 2.1 reduce to thirty-five effect sizes in table 2.2.

7. The best known findings, those reported by Ansolabehere and Iyengar (1995), are not far removed from a mean effect size of zero. Ansolabehere and Iyengar found that viewing a single negative ad (compared with viewing a single positive ad) decreased intention to vote in the upcoming election by about 4.2 percent. With more than 2,200 subjects in the analysis, this effect is statistically significant ($p < .05$) but very "noisy," and it translates into an effect size of only $-.10$—that is, one-tenth of a standard deviation.

8. With the same set of assumptions, it would take four additional studies of the effects of negative political advertising on turnout, with average effect sizes of -1.0, to reverse our conclusion about Ansolabehere and Iyengar's demobilization hypothesis that negative advertising, if anything, increases turnout.

9. The statistics reported in this paragraph are for unadjusted effect sizes. None of the conclusions changed when we examined the adjusted effect sizes. (See appendix B for further explanation of these adjustments.)

10. Interestingly, although advertising practitioners perceive comparative ads for commercial products as effective and are making increasingly frequent use of such ads (Rogers and Williams 1989), the research literature indicates that comparative ads are generally no more effective than other ads at generating favorable attitudes toward products and intentions to purchase them (e.g., Barry 1993). The result is a gap between research and practice in product advertising that closely parallels what we have observed for negative political advertising.

Who Uses Negative Campaigning?

3

NEGATIVE CAMPAIGNING has a bad reputation. Critics find it widespread, unfair, and harmful to the political process. To put the practice in context, we begin with newspaper portraits of three senatorial campaigns in 2000 that exhibited variations in negative campaigning.

The first race, for an open seat in New York, pitted Hillary Rodham Clinton, soon to leave the White House with the president, her husband, against Rick Lazio, a Republican congressman from the suburbs. A reporter (Siegel 2000) describes some of the exchanges in a race that would ultimately cost $80 million:

> Hours after the Lazio campaign launched an ad featuring a testimonial by his wife, the Clinton campaign answered with a spot portraying the Suffolk County congressman as being in the pocket of special interests. It begins with a clip of Rick Lazio saying, "Show me your friends . . . and I'll tell you who you are."
>
> The ad then cites a *Daily News* article that revealed he took at least $1 million in contributions from the homebuilding industry his congressional panel regulates. "And Lazio's tried to help them weaken safety and construction standards," the ad says.
>
> The candidates also dueled in a second set of TV ads aimed at female voters.
>
> After the Clinton campaign launched a spot starring Rep. Nita Lowey (D-Westchester) vouching for the First Lady's record of accomplishments, Team Lazio responded with an ad that begins, "You know, there's something about Hillary."
>
> "She's smart, God knows she's aching to be senator, but I wonder what she'd do in Washington," the announcer says.
>
> The women in the ad then say Clinton pushed a health plan that was a "disaster" and would hike taxes as senator.
>
> The ad ends with a woman saying of Lazio, "Sure, he's a scrappy guy. But, hey, that's New York."

The campaign was quite different in North Dakota, where Republican Duane Sand challenged incumbent Kent Conrad, although negative comments were still evident (Canton 2000):

North Dakota's Republican candidate for the U.S. Senate said Monday in Bismarck that Freedom to Farm was a failed policy, and he proposed seven tools to remedy the ailing national farm policy.

Sand claimed his program would double commodity prices within 10 years.

"Decoupling government control from the farmer at the local level, we've got to keep that. But there are some big problems with Freedom to Farm," Sand said. . . . But he said the program failed because the Clinton administration has neglected to use its executive powers to enforce trade laws. . . .

Sand's Democratic opponent, incumbent Sen. Kent Conrad, accused Sand in a written statement of sidestepping the larger issue of Freedom to Farm, which Conrad described as "disastrous."

"That's like talking about the sinking of the Titanic without mentioning the iceberg," he said.

Conrad again pointed to his Farm Income and Trade Equity bill, which would provide U.S. farmers subsidies keyed to those given European farmers by the European Union.

Sand hammered away, as he has throughout the campaign season, at Conrad's FITE bill: "Let's be realistic. My opponent's farm proposal is languishing in committee. He doesn't have the political power to get it to the floor. We've got to have access to the chairmen of those committees."

Conrad also said Sand had borrowed from his agenda, notably a crop insurance bill that will go into law in October.

In the same election year, a very different campaign was waged in Virginia, where the Republican governor, George Allen, challenged incumbent Democrat Charles Robb (Melton and Morin 2000):

The Nov. 7 election is as much a referendum on Robb's 12 years in the Senate—a tepid two terms, say even many Democrats—as it is about Allen's tough-minded brand of conservatism.

"I'm not impressed with Robb—he's the invisible man of the Senate," said Thomas Kerwin, 70, of Arlington, retired treasurer of the Norfolk Southern railroad.

"But the abortion issue has become sort of a hot topic in the last week or so, so now I'm leaning toward him," Kerwin said. "It's none of the government's business what a woman does with her own body. It's that simple. Allen's going off in the wrong direction. He's fairly far over to the right." . . .

But Allen has paid careful attention to those suburbs, spending millions of dollars on upbeat, localized ads and campaigning there in person nearly every recent weekend. . . .

Meanwhile, Allen's signature issue, a $ 1,000-per-child educational tax credit, seems to have suffered under Robb's relentless pounding of the proposal, which the Democrat says is merely a precursor to private school vouchers. . . .

Some voters said Allen won their support by projecting a more positive image, adding in some cases that the Republican may be better suited to a Senate that seems likely to remain in the GOP's control.

"He seems to be straightforward," said Howard Eichler, 67, of Reston, who has already voted for the Republican by absentee ballot. "His promises are better—he'll be able to follow through."

Robb supporters said they were wary of Allen's agenda and temperament. Carolyn Ward, 68, a longtime Arlington resident who used to work as a contracting officer for the Defense Department, said she is voting for Robb in part because she saw gaps in a publicly funded safety net when she nursed her paralyzed mother for eight years. . . .

Ward also said Allen's personality was too abrasive. . . .

Allen's temperament aside, voters were sharply divided about whether Robb deserves to be reelected to a third six-year term. . . . Some Democrats and unaligned voters sounded torn in describing their feelings about Robb and the race, determined to deny Allen the Senate seat but wistful about what Robb could have accomplished with it. Robb "doesn't jump off a lot, and maybe that's not the best strategy," Ward said.

Allen partisans said they welcomed a referendum on Robb.

As these portraits illustrate, negative campaigning can be person- or issue-related, focused on a candidate's record or his or her promises, and vicious or informative. The results also vary: Democrat Clinton won her open seat, incumbent Democrat Conrad won an easy reelection, but Democrat Robb was defeated.

Politicians therefore use negative campaigning not because they are evil or mean-spirited but because they believe it helps them win elections. Prominent Republican and Democratic consultants agree:

> Voters will tell you in focus groups that they don't like negative ads, but they retain the information so much better than the positive ones. The point is: People like dirty laundry. Why do tabloids sell? (Roger Stone, Republican consultant, in Colford 1986, p. 104)

Candidates engage in negative campaigning because it works. No matter how much people say they dislike it, negative campaigns continue to move voters from one column to the other. (Susan Estrich, 1988 Dukakis campaign manager, 1993, p. 11A)

In this chapter, we probe basic initial questions. How much negative campaigning is there in Senate contests? How do they compare to other elections? Who does it? Under what conditions? Can we predict which campaigns will be more negative? Before we despair for the future of the American republic, we should know what is actually happening.

Formal theory provides hints about when candidates logically *should* employ negative campaigning (Skaperdas and Grofman 1995; Theilmann and Wilhite 1998), and reports from campaign consultants provide empirical data when they *would* "go negative" in hypothetical situations (Perloff and Kinsey 1992). But there is little beyond anecdotal evidence from single elections about what candidates actually have *done* in real campaigns.[1]

For example, studies of the televised political advertisements produced by the major presidential candidates since 1960 (Geer 1998; Jamieson and Waldman 1997; Kaid and Johnston 1991) report the percentage of attack ads (or negative themes within the ads). But, because we do not know how often these different advertisements were shown, it is hard to be precise about the nature of the *campaigns* from a coding of the advertisements.[2]

The best evidence on campaign conduct—but still confined to the presidential level—is Goldstein's (1997a, 1997b) studies of negative advertising during the 1996 campaign (see also Freedman and Goldstein 1999; Goldstein and Freedman 2000, 2002a, 2002b). Utilizing new technology to monitor satellite transmissions, Goldstein provides detailed knowledge of the airing of political commercials in the seventy-five largest media markets in the United States. For 1996, Goldstein reports that 27 percent of Clinton's spots and 71 percent of Dole's spots were largely negative or "attack" (i.e., opponent-focused), 66 percent of Clinton's spots and 15 percent of Dole's spots were "contrast," and the remainder were primarily positive or "advocacy."

The most extensive evidence about the degree of negative campaigning in U.S. congressional elections has been gathered by Tinkham and Weaver-Lariscy (1991; Weaver-Lariscy and Tinkham 1996), who surveyed candidates in competitive House races after the 1982 and 1990 congressional elections. Although we are somewhat skeptical about the reliability of self-reports of these behaviors, particularly gathered after an election, their findings show that about 7 percent of the candidates claimed to have run primarily negative campaigns in 1982, with another 41 percent of the campaigns classified as "comparative" (i.e., stressing issue stands and/or personal characteristics of both the candidate *and* the opponent). Thus roughly half of the campaigns involved some admitted attacks on the opponent. In 1990, the figures were 8 percent and 27 percent, respectively.

It is not clear how representative these findings are,[3] but Ansolabehere et al. (1994) report roughly comparable data from the 1992 Senate elections. Using newspaper reports of the Senate elections, these authors classified 34 percent of the Senate campaigns as primarily negative, with another 17 percent coded as having a "mixed" tone.[4] Kahn and Kenney (1999b) examined a sample of political advertisements from the 1988 to 1992 Senate elections stored in the Political Commercial Archive at the University of Oklahoma. They calculate that 59 percent of the commercials they examined were advocacy, with the remainder a mix of attack and comparative.

We seek to extend this research by broadening our view of campaigns beyond television advertising and by examining a wider set of election campaigns. For these purposes, we examine negative campaigning by the two major-party candidates in virtually all contested U.S. Senate elections from 1992 through 2002. We address two major descriptive questions, the extent and the incidence of negative campaigning in Senate contests.

Negative Campaigning: How Much?

Figure 3.1 gives an overall picture of negative campaigning by both major-party Senate candidates between 1992 and 2002. During the time period under study, overall negative campaigning varied between a low of 27.8 per-

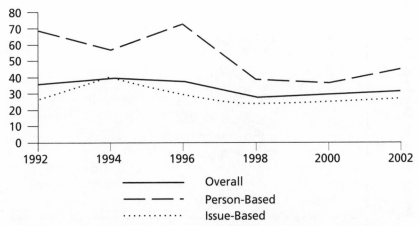

Figure 3.1   Percent Negativism in U.S. Senate Election Campaigns, 1992–2002

Note: Data average across the Democratic and Republican campaigns, with each party's figures weighted by the proportion of total spending controlled by each candidate. The overall numbers in the figure are a similarly weighted average of the percent issue-based and person-based negativism from each candidate, now also weighted by the relative proportion of all statements falling into those two categories.

cent in 1998 and a high of 39.7 percent in 1994 (when the Republicans took control of the Senate), with an overall mean of about 33.7 percent. There is no systematic trend for changes in negative campaigning over time, at least as estimated by our data.

Figure 3.2 is another look at these same data, now ignoring election year and focusing on races where the incumbent was seeking reelection. The percent of negative campaigning by the incumbent candidate is plotted on the vertical axis, while the percent of negative campaigning by the opposing challenger is plotted on the horizontal axis. Now one can see the individual data points and get a better sense of the actual level of campaign negativism in the various Senate elections. As indicated by the mean levels of negative campaigning reported in figure 3.1, most of these data points are in the lower left-hand quadrant of the figure. About a dozen incumbents engaged in no negative campaigning that we could detect, as did one challenger. And while there is a moderate positive slope to these data, in general there appears to be a great deal of variation across races.

Our results document that negative campaigning is clearly evident, although not predominant, in U.S. Senate elections between 1992 and 2002.

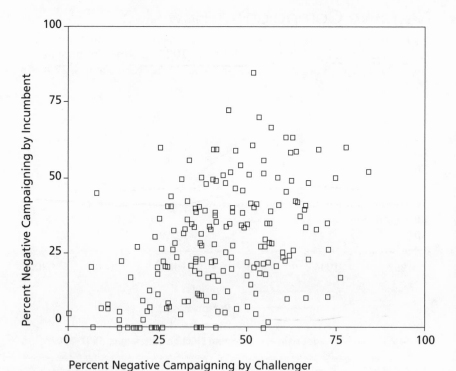

Figure 3.2   Negative Campaigning in U.S. Senate Elections

Across the six election years and 192 election campaigns we considered, about a third of the comments attributed to the major-party campaigns were negative—that is, they concerned the opponent. This figure is roughly comparable to the results Tinkham and Weaver-Lariscy (1991; Weaver-Lariscy and Tinkham 1996) report from the 1982 and 1990 congressional elections but considerably less than Goldstein (1997a, 1997b) reports for the 1996 presidential election.

Two plausible reasons explain some of the differences. First, in the case of the 1996 presidential election, one of the candidates was widely expected to lose and, consistent with our results, he did engage in an inordinate amount of negative campaigning. Second, Goldstein's data are exclusively from political commercials, while ours address campaigns more broadly. It may be easier for candidates to attack their opponents in television commercials than in more personal contexts, such as a public speech or an interview. If so, then our data probably underestimate the negativism of the televised political commercials from these Senate elections. By the same token, however, judgments about the nature of *the campaign* based solely on evidence from political ads probably overstate the level of negativism in the campaign. And we have already argued that presidential elections are different in kind from elections for other offices.

Negative Campaigning: Who Does It?

We test seven hypotheses that represent the strategic decisions of candidates and consultants in the American campaign environment, and most of these maxims would also apply to other countries. These hypotheses are based on a core theory of candidates as rational actors who chose campaign strategies instrumentally as they seek electoral victory. Any campaign strategy must be based on information available before (and during) the campaign; it must also reflect the relative availability of scarce resources (particularly money). We assume rational actors will employ negative campaigning to the extent they believe it is an efficient means to reach their electoral goal.

Derived from these basic premises and the extant literature, we expect relatively greater use of negative campaigning in specific situations, particularly the following:

1. *Candidates who are behind* in the race or who expect to lose will employ more negative campaigning (Haynes and Rhine 1998; Kahn and Kenney 1999b; Karrh and Halpern 1997; Skaperdas and Grofman 1995). This hypothesis assumes that candidates generally believe going negative is a risky but potentially very effective strategy. Candidates who attack their opponents should lower evaluations of the target of their attacks but might also suffer a backlash and see their own

evaluations fall as well. Uncertainty about which candidate will ulti-mately suffer more—the target or the sponsor of the attacks—is where the risk comes. Candidates who are behind or who expect to lose can accept the risk more easily than candidates who are ahead.

2. *Candidates in close elections* will be more willing to engage in signifi-cant amounts of negative campaigning because negative campaigning is generally believed to be an effective, if risky, strategy (Garramone 1984, 1985; Hale, Fox, and Farmer 1996; Mann and Ornstein 1983). The logic of this prediction is similar to the first and relies on the same set of beliefs about the potential gains and losses from negative cam-paigning. If the election looks like it will be close, and the gains from attacking the opponent seem more certain (and more immediate) than the possibility of voter backlash, then candidates will have increased motivation to go negative.

3. *Challengers*, with no office to lose, similarly will be more willing to bear any downside risks of negative campaigning (Guskind and Hags-trom 1988; Hale, Fox, and Farmer 1996; Kahn and Kenney 1999b; Kaid and Davidson 1986; Tinkham and Weaver-Lariscy 1995). Beat-ing an incumbent is a longshot anyway, and many challengers believe that their only chance is to give the electorate some reason to vote against the sitting incumbent.

4. *Candidates with relatively fewer campaign resources* than their oppo-nents will be more likely to engage in negative campaigning (Jamieson 1992; Johnson-Cartee and Copeland 1991; Pfau and Kenski 1990). The assumption here is that negative campaigning is a quick and effi-cient way to make a dent in the relative standing of two candidates in an election. They can't get their own messages across this way, but candidates who need to get "more bang for the buck" from their lim-ited campaign resources may believe that going negative is a relatively efficacious way to campiaign.

5. *Republican candidates*, all else equal, will be more likely to use nega-tive campaigning. This prediction is based on the preferred strategies of Republican consultants, who more often report they would attack their opponents in certain campaign situations (Perloff and Kinsey 1992), and the greater acceptance among Republican voters, com-pared with Democrats, of attacking the opponent as a campaign strategy.[5]

6. *Men* will engage more in negative campaigning than will women. It is difficult to make a firm prediction on the effect of candidate gender. On the one hand, common sex stereotypes suggest males are generally more aggressive than females, implying that men would be more likely to employ negative campaigning (Trent and Sabourin 1993). On the other hand, women may want to show they are "tough enough" to

make it in a traditionally male occupation by using the same campaign techniques as men (Schultz and Pancer 1997) and may even feel compelled to "out-tough" their male oppoenents. There is some evidence for both of these points of view. On balance, we expect a real, but not large, gender difference (Procter, Schenck-Hamlin, and Haase 1994), with male candidates being slightly more likely than female candidates to attack their opponents.

7. *Candidates responding to opponents* engaging in negative campaigning will themselves employ more negative campaigning (Haynes and Rhine 1998; Kahn and Kenney 1999b). The lesson that every political consultant seems to have learned from Michael Dukakis's 1988 presidential campaign (indeed, the lesson they all claim to have known all along) is that a candidate must respond to attacks by the opponent. To borrow an acronym from international relations, campaigns are thus predicted to exhibit MAD, or mutual assured detraction (see also Roddy and Garramone 1988). If we had to choose one hypothesis that we were most certain would be supported by the data, this would be our bet.

Results

We now examine the effects of a candidate's strategic decisions on levels of campaign negativism, as specified in the seven previously listed hypotheses. As a first step, we calculate the simple bivariate relationship between the independent variable dictated by each hypothesis and the proportion of a candidate's campaigning that was negative. The results of these bivariate analyses are summarized in table 3.1 and figures 3.3 to 3.6. For categorical independent variables—candidate status, party, and candidate gender—we compare mean levels of negative campaigning. For interval-level independent variables—normal vote outcome, expected closeness, relative campaign spending, and opponent's negativism—we calculate the Pearson correlation with negative campaigning.

As expected, negative campaigning was *more* likely if the candidate was a challenger or in an open-seat contest, Republican, male (see figure 3.3), engaged in a race expected to be close (see figure 3.4), and facing an opponent's negative campaign (see figure 3.6). On the other hand, the negative strategy was *less* likely among incumbents (see figure 3.3), in projected runaway races (see figure 3.4), and among well-financed candidates (see figure 3.5). These findings confirm all of our hypotheses, at least at the bivariate level, although the effects are not as monotonic as the hypotheses suggest.[6]

While these initial results provide strong support for the seven hypotheses, the various explanatory variables are hardly independent of each other. To determine which of these variables has the greatest independent effect on

Table 3.1   Who Uses Negative Campaigning? A First Look

Mean Level of Negative Campaigning	
Incumbent (N = 143)	29.7%
Open Seat (N = 98)	39.5%
Challenger (N = 143)	41.4%
$F_{(2,381)}$ = 19.69***	
Democrats (N = 192)	34.6%
Republicans (N = 192)	38.5%
$t_{(382)}$ = 2.20**	
Males (N = 329)	37.1%
Females (N = 55)	32.9%
$t_{(382)}$ = 1.65*	

Correlation of Use of Negative Campaigning with:	
Expected Vote Outcome	$-$.29***
Expected Closeness of Race	.20***
Relative Campaign Spending	$-$.30***
Opponent's Negative Campaigning	.31***

N = 384.
*p < .05   **p < .02   ***p < .001
Note: All hypothesis tests are directional, so one-tailed statistical tests are employed.

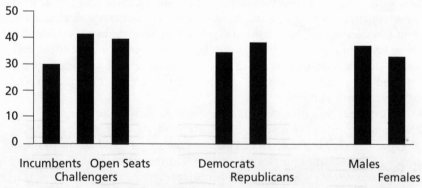

Figure 3.3   Impact of Incumbency, Party, and Candidate Gender on Percent Negative Campaigning

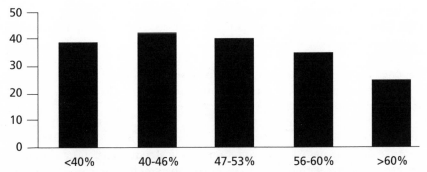

Figure 3.4   Impact of Expected Outcome of the Race on Percent Negative Campaigning

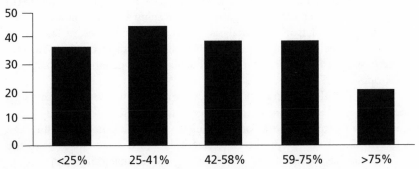

Figure 3.5   Impact of Relative Campaign Resources on Percent Negative Campaigning

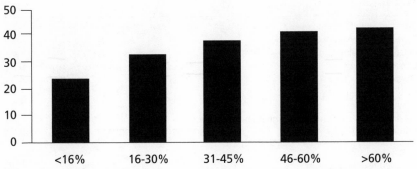

Figure 3.6   Impact of Opponent's Campaign Negativism on Percent Negative Campaigning

predicting use of negative campaigning, we turn to a multivariate analysis. Our measure of negative campaigning is regressed on the previous independent variables, along with five dummy variables representing election year. The inclusion of the amount of negative campaigning by the candidate's opponent as an independent variable in this analysis makes the use of OLS regression inappropriate, however, as this predictor is clearly endogenous. Instead, we employ 2SLS analysis, as described in appendix B.

Three variables stand out as particularly important in the multivariate analysis. Controlling for other variables in the equation, as seen in table 3.2, negative campaigning is more common among Republicans, more common among candidates with relatively less money than their opponents, and more common among those who face negative campaigning opponents. All else equal, the campaigns of Republicans are about 9 percent more negative than the campaigns of Democrats. An increase in one point in the percentage of campaign funds a candidate has (relative to his or her opponent) results in about a fifth of a percent less negative campaigning by the candidate. Furthermore, it is clear from this analysis that Senate candidates, at least from 1992 to 2002, believed they had to retaliate against attacks on almost a one-to-one basis, as can be seen in the .86 coefficient on negative campaigning by the opponent.[7]

The results also contradict some conventional wisdom of campaign experts. Once other factors are controlled, expecting to lose (or win) is not significantly related to more (or less) negative campaigning, although the coefficient does have the predicted sign. Similarly, expected closeness of the race does not have a significant effect on negative campaigning. Apparently,

Table 3.2   A Multivariate Analysis of the Use of Negative Campaigning by U.S. Senate Candidates

	B	S.E.
Expected Vote Outcome	−.35	.24
Expected Closeness of Race	.13	.41
Relative Campaign Spending	−.22***	.06
Challenger	4.12	5.23
Open Seat	1.55	4.03
Party (Republican)	8.89***	2.29
Female Candidate	−.18	2.67
Relative Use of Negative Campaigning by Opponent	.86**	.26
Constant	27.01*	15.98
N		382
Adjusted R²		.20

$*p < .05$ $**p < .01$ $***p < .001$
Note: Table entries are unstandardized 2SLS coefficients. Analysis also included dummy variables for election year, none of which were significant.

candidates are not necessarily driven to the attack by intimations of electoral mortality. The combination of findings suggests the importance of the immediate campaign environment, rather than any general handbook of campaign rationality. Candidates do think strategically, but locally, as they view the projected outcomes of their races, their opponents' efforts, and their relative finances.

Finally, the interesting gender difference found earlier in the bivariate analysis disappears in the multivariate analysis. Certainly in these data, female candidates were somewhat more likely to be Democrats (twenty-eight of the forty-nine were, or 57 percent), which would account for some of their lower level of negative campaigning. And if female candidates were frequently "sacrificial lambs" who had no real chance of winning, then they probably faced opponents who engaged in much less negative campaigning, which would result in less reciprocal negative campaigning by women. In any case, once these factors are controlled, the mean differences we observed at the bivariate level disappear.

Implications

The analyses in this chapter add to our skepticism over the conventional wisdom on negative campaigning, reinforcing the conclusions reached in chapter 2. Although negative campaigning is widespread, it does not predominate in Senate elections, and there is no evident increase in the practice during the past decade. Moreover, those who practice campaign negativism are different in important respects from common expectations.

Going beyond our data, these results also allow some speculation about other campaigns, both within and outside of the United States. We have every reason to expect that most, even all, American campaigns would demonstrate the same behaviors. The academic literature on campaigning makes few distinctions among offices (e.g., Salmore and Salmore 1989), and candidates too probably follow the same strategies from one contest to another. Senate candidates are often the same persons who have sought, or will seek, power in races for governors, Congress, state legislatures, and city councils. They are nominated by the same parties, use the services of the same consultants, and receive contributions from the same donors. The lessons they learn and the behaviors they exhibit in one race are likely to be replicated in other contests.

Obvious and major differences exist between American elections and those in other nations, and this admittedly limited, possibly parochial, analysis cannot be casually extended to electoral studies more generally. There still may be reasons, however, to consider these findings in research on other democracies, even as we recognize the great variation in party systems, electoral laws, and political cultures.

On a theoretical level, the strategic choices that lead to negative campaigning will face candidates as rational actors in any competitive environment. Empirically, party systems throughout the democratic world increasingly share many of the characteristics of American parties and replicate many of the campaign behaviors of American politicians (see Holtz-Bacha, Kaid, and Johnston 1994 on similarities in political advertisements). In political practice, this convergence of candidate behavior is furthered by the internationalization of the political trade, as illustrated by the involvement of such American campaign consultants as Roger Ailes and James Carville in elections in Britain, Israel, and other nations.

These findings, even if restricted to U.S. Senate elections, also carry implications for the reform of campaigns, particularly restrictions on negative campaigning. Even if such restrictions were normatively desirable—a subject we consider in the concluding chapter—they would be difficult to achieve in practice. The reality is that campaign strategies, including the use of negative tactics, are deliberately chosen by aspirants to office. It makes sense for challengers and those with less money to resort to the presumed efficacy of negative campaigning in order to overcome the wider reputation and deeper pockets of their opponents. It certainly makes sense for candidates under attack to reply in kind to their opponents. These are rational, not random, patterns.

On the other hand, there is no evident political reason for men to be more aggressive and negative in their campaigns. Our analysis shows that, at least in these races, biology is not destiny and testosterone does not dominate electoral judgment. Both men and women choose their strategies for political, not hormonal, reasons. Even the Republican proclivity toward negative campaigning may have a political foundation, derived from the party's ties to consultants who have used these methods successfully. It may also derive from the fundamental Republican hostility to governmental power. Not trusting government generally, candidates of the party may be more ready to criticize the holders and aspirants to government office.

Since negative campaigning is largely a rational course of action for political candidates, we cannot expect spontaneous change in this behavior. Certainly, admonitions to "be good" are as unlikely to be effective with candidates as they are with children who find cookies in places their parents have designated "off limits." We can understand politics most easily if we consider candidates as self-interested and also accept the theoretical premise, however exaggerated in reality, that "they act solely in order to attain the income, prestige, and power which come from being in office" (Downs 1957, 28). As John Aldrich (1995, 24) wrote about politicians' relationships with parties and their employment of negative campaigning, they "use its powers, resources, and institutional forms when they believe doing so increases their prospects for winning desired outcomes, and they turn from it if it does not."

The patterns of negative campaigning parallel the wants and opportunities of practicing politicians. As we will see in the following chapters, negative campaigning has fewer deleterious effects than commonly claimed. Furthermore, as we will contend in chapter 7, it even has some desirable aspects. But, whether effective or not, desirable or dangerous, it will likely continue unless change also satisfies those needs and opens those opportunities.

Notes

This chapter is based on Richard R. Lau and Gerald M. Pomper, "Negative Campaigning by U.S. Senate Candidates," *Party Politics* 7 (January 2001): 69–87.

1. Shaw (1999) presents detailed evidence on how strongly or frequently presidential candidates campaigned in each state (i.e., how much they spent on advertising in each state, the number of visits they made to each state) but has no evidence on the nature of the campaigns conducted in each state (i.e., what candidates said or did when they were in the state), which is our focus here.

2. For example, Goldstein (1997a, 1997b) reports that while 40 percent of Dole's overall 1996 campaign advertisements were advocacy, only 15 percent of the spots that were *run* were advocacy.

3. The response rate for the two surveys combined was a little under 50 percent.

4. Ansolabehere et al. (1994) do not report their data separately for the different candidates.

5. Education is often seen as a key mediating factor, as more educated people are presumably more familiar with seeing intellectual criticisms and debates. Republicans tend to have more formal education than Democrats.

6. For example, as seen in figure 3.5, the highest level of campaign negativism is displayed not by candidates with the fewest resources but by candidates in the second quintile, who have significantly fewer resources than their opponents but still have enough money to make a real go of it.

7. The strength of this last coefficient is particularly noteworthy, given that it is based on a pretty weak first-stage estimate of the opponent's campaign tone (see appendix B).

The Effectiveness of Negative Campaigning

4

N EGATIVE CAMPAIGNING is common, yet its effect is uncertain. Consider two examples from the earlier years of our study. The first race came in California in 1992 (Gunnison and Wildermuth 1992):

> One of the hardest-hitting television ads of the fall was aired this weekend by Republican Senator John Seymour, who is running against Dianne Feinstein.
>
> "Dianne Feinstein is a candidate again. And now she claims to support the death penalty. But since my son was murdered by Robert Alton Harris, I've kept a close eye on these politicians," San Diego Police Detective Steve Baker says in the ad.
>
> In April, Harris became the first man to be executed in California in nearly a quarter of a century. He murdered Baker's son and another teenage boy in 1978.
>
> "And the fact is, when Feinstein had a chance, she paroled 21 convicted murderers," Baker says, speaking to the camera in a prison setting.
>
> "We don't need another liberal senator like Feinstein—appointing more liberal judges and turning people loose like Robert Alton Harris," Baker concludes.
>
> Feinstein supporters were outraged.
>
> "It is rather remarkable that Senator Seymour would feel the need to politically exploit this grief for his own re-election purposes," said E. F. Murphy, vice president of the Peace Officers Research Association, which backs Feinstein.
>
> Feinstein spokesman Kam Kuwata called the ad "a piece of trash that demeans the office of a U.S. senator." Democratic National Committee Chairman Ron Brown called it "desperate."

Despite the negative attack, challenger Feinstein won the race. In North Carolina four years later, another Democratic challenger encountered attacks from a Republican incumbent (Nowell 1996):

> Democrat Harvey Gantt vowed Wednesday to answer a new television ad by Republican Jesse Helms that injects the issues of race and affirmative action into their U.S. Senate campaign. . . .

Gantt was referring to an ad from the Helms campaign that contends Gantt's minority status allowed him preferential treatment in landing a new broadcast license and building contracts for his architectural firm.

The Helms ad, which was unveiled this week, said: "In 1986, Harvey Gantt used his minority status to purchase interest in a TV station under false pretense. . . . Weeks later, he and his partners sold the station to a white-owned corporation, making millions."

The ad also said Gantt got "preferential treatment on public school contracts." . . .

Pressed Wednesday to divulge his strategy to respond to the attack from Helms, Gantt played it close to the vest.

"You'll have to watch what we do," he said. "I'm not going to tell you what we're going to do until we do it."

Whatever his intended strategy, Gantt failed to respond effectively, as Helms was reelected to his fifth term. Sometimes negative campaigning appears to work.

Negative campaigning may be on the rise because it is generally presumed that these methods, particularly in the form of televised advertising, are an unusually effective means of campaigning, a real advantage to those candidates who have the backbone to employ it. Social psychological theory provides several reasons why negative information ought to be more persuasive than comparable positive information (Kanouse and Hanson 1972). Lau (1982, 1985) groups these reasons into two main categories. The first is perceptual: Negative information may be more likely than comparable positive information to be noticed and processed, thereby having the opportunity to get its message across. The second reason is motivational, based on the greater survival benefits resulting from avoiding costs rather than approaching gains. Less formally, some negative campaigning may be advantageous to candidates (particularly "untested" challengers) if it helps convey the impression that they are "tough enough" to be leaders.

There are significant methodological difficulties in specifying campaign effects of *any* type (Bartels 1993). Indeed, a considerable amount of research in political science argues that the context in which the election is held (e.g., the state of the economy, the popularity of the incumbent president), rather than the campaign itself, is what really matters (Lewis-Beck and Rice 1992; Rosenstone 1983). Of course, these macro-level explanations were put forth only after several major attempts to determine the influence of political campaigns had failed to detect any influence at all (see Holbrook 1996 for a review of this literature). More recently, researchers have been able to provide convincing evidence that political campaigns do have some detectable effects, although the typical study looks for fairly specific, and therefore fairly limited, effects.

In past studies of Senate elections, one important variable has been missing from the analyses. Any candidate, even one blessed with a large campaign war chest and other advantages, can campaign wisely or poorly. We do not pretend to measure all of the strategic decisions that any candidate must make during an election campaign. We can, however, measure one important strategic decision that surely shapes many particular campaign behaviors: Should I emphasize my own abilities, accomplishments, and policy stands? Or should I concentrate on attacking my opponent on these grounds? Individual campaigns will include both approaches, but they will combine them in different proportions. Simply put, candidates will vary in their relative use of negative campaigning. We seek to examine the effect of that variation.

The ability of negative campaigning to affect the vote decision has rarely been put to a convincing test. This chapter attempts a fuller analysis of elections involving incumbents seeking reelection; the next chapter will deal with open-seat races. In both, we will address a very simple research question in the context of U.S. Senate contests: How effective is negative campaigning in winning elections?

To answer this simple question, however, we must do some complex investigation. To consider the effects of negative campaigning, we first need to resolve problems of endogeneity, or interactive causality, in the political process and in our methods. In appendix B we discuss our solution to this problem, 2SLS analysis, which produces estimates of the problematic spending and campaign tone variables that have been "purged" of their statistical problems. Here we begin to consider the product of all of this statistical work: reliable estimates of the true effects of campaign spending (although it is not our focus) and tone (our major interest) on the outcome of Senate elections. But we will also consider the costs of this technique: less efficient measures of these same problematic variables.

Does It Work?: Aggregate Analysis

We begin our exploration of the effectiveness of negative campaigning by considering our aggregate state-level data set. Table 4.1 reports five separate analyses of four different models predicting percent vote for the incumbent senator, the first two without any of our measures of campaign tone, the others with different indicators of incumbent and challenger negativism. The table presents two different estimates of the baseline model, the first produced by ordinary least squares (OLS) regression, which ignores the problems of endogeneity, and the second produced by 2SLS, which attempts to eliminate them. Although we are primarily concerned with the effects of the campaign tone variables, we will briefly comment on our base model, which

Table 4.1 Percent Vote for Incumbent Senator, State Level, 1992–2002

| | OLS | | 2SLS | | | | | | | |
| | Base Model | | Base Model | | Model 1 | | Model 2 | | Model 3 | |
	B	S.E.	B	S.E.	B	S.E.	B	S.E.	B	S.E.
Constant	63.57***	2.41	55.53***	4.87	71.95***	6.59	58.85***	8.54	63.01***	8.78
Presidential Popularity	.13**	.05	.04	.06	−.02	.06	−.03	.04	−.02	.04
Midterm Election	−.29	.84	−.47	1.09	1.33	1.14	1.24@	.73	1.17@	.68
State Partisanship	.14**	.05	.08	.06	.18**	.07	.17***	.04	.17***	.04
State Change in PCDI	.31	.38	.29	.41	−.28	.45	−.16	.29	−.15	.27
Incumbent Scandal	1.18	3.66	−.96	3.91	.91	4.03	.81	2.78	.76	2.46
Incumbent Controversy	−1.44	1.93	−1.58	2.77	3.08	3.02	2.82	1.96	3.19@	1.85
Incumbent Health Problems	−3.24	3.73	−3.90	4.32	−2.47	4.40	−2.12	2.84	−2.31	2.64
Challenger a Governor	−7.69**	3.37	−7.10	4.55	−2.47	4.75	−1.69	3.08	−1.47	2.82
Challenger Major Office	−4.29**	1.70	−2.50	2.31	−.35	2.45	−.62	1.58	−.54	1.48
Challenger in House	−7.33***	1.78	−5.14@	2.97	−1.62	3.17	−2.05	1.95	−1.75	1.96
Challenger Minor Office	−2.78@	1.58	−.97	1.71	−1.86	1.76	−1.68	1.13	−1.69	1.05
Incumbent Spending	4.77***	1.67	3.55*	1.68	3.16@	1.72	9.21***	2.50	7.93**	2.60
Challenger Spending	−11.52***	1.79	−3.29@	1.70	−3.18@	1.73	−7.38***	1.96	−8.35***	2.02
Incumbent Negativism					−.25***	.07	.33	.21	.19	.23
Challenger Negativism					−.11	.08	−.32***	.10	−.37**	.11
Incumbent Neg. × Spending							−.17*	.06	−.11	.08
Challenger Neg. × Spending							.10**	.04	.15*	.06
Weighted Inc. Negativism × Weighted Chal. Negativism									−.000	.000
Adjusted R²	.42		.25		.34		.35		.35	
Standard Error	6.92		7.86		7.41		7.34		7.36	

@ p < .10   * p < .05   ** p < .01   *** p < .001

Note: Except for the first two columns, table entries are 2SLS coefficients. Weighted incumbent and challenger negativism are negativism multiplied by spending. N = 141.

excludes them. This also gives us the opportunity to see the effects of employing a 2SLS procedure.

A quick comparison of the two different estimates of the base model reveals the primary cost of a 2SLS procedure: less *efficient* estimate of all the coefficients. All but one of the standard errors of the 2SLS estimates are larger than those produced by OLS. The increase is as much as 50 percent, which is considerable. Likewise, the adjusted R-square (R^2), a measure of how much of the variance in the dependent variable is explained by the equation, decreases from .42 to .25, while the standard error of the estimate increases by about 14 percent.[1] It is probably best to look at the OLS estimates to determine which of the control variables truly makes a difference, while relying on the 2SLS estimates for the spending and campaign tone variables.

To begin with the national factors, presidential popularity does help the electoral chances of incumbents from the president's party seeking reelection, but they are not hurt significantly during off-year elections, when the president's party typically loses seats in Congress. We estimate that an eight point increase in the popularity of the president will result in a one point increase in the share of the two-party vote received by incumbent senators of the president's party. These first two coefficients have their expected sign, but they present a mixed picture of the effect of national factors on the outcome of Senate elections.

Among the local factors, statewide partisanship clearly affects the reelection chances of incumbents. For every percent that the number of partisans of an incumbent's party exceeds the number of partisans of a challenger's party, the incumbent gets about one-seventh of a point boost at the polls. On the other hand, state change in per capita disposable income, while positively signed as expected, has no true impact: Incumbent senators do not reliably receive any credit for good economic conditions in their states.[2] As most of them have very little effect on their states' economies, one way or another, this nonsignificant result seems valid to us.

All of the candidate-specific factors should have negative signs in the equation, and all but the first (incumbent scandal) do. Controlling on other variables in the equation, however, none of the three indicators of some weakness in the incumbent approach statistical significance. The statistical problem for us (although not for the incumbents!) is that too few of the incumbents get involved in some scandal or controversy, or suffer from some serious health problem at election time. As a result there is little variance in any of these dummy variables. On the other hand, all four of the indicators of the quality of the challenger significantly improve the challenger's chances of winning. Compared with challengers with no electoral experience,[3] ex- or sitting governors and (typically) current members of the House of Representatives seeking election to the Senate do 7 to 8 percent better at the polls, according to our estimates; other major statewide office holders (e.g., lieutenant governors) do about four points better, and even minor office holders (e.g., city mayors) do almost three points better (see Jacobson and Kernell 1983; Squire 1989).

The major difference between the OLS and 2SLS estimates of the baseline model concerns the effect of candidate spending. The OLS procedure reveals the standard finding: Challenger spending is much more important than incumbent spending (almost two and a half times more important). Following Gerber (1998), however, we would argue those figures are wrong. The 2SLS procedure produces much more reliable estimates. Money matters, of course, but by our estimates it matters just about as much for incumbents as it does for challengers.

In this book we are primarily interested in the effects of a campaign's tone. Models 1, 2, and 3 all include indicators of the negativism of the incumbent's and challenger's campaigns. If attacking the opponent is an effective campaign strategy, then the campaign tone variables ought to have a positive sign for the incumbent and a negative sign for the challenger.

Model 1 simply adds our measures of the negativism of each campaign to the analysis. The results suggest that "going negative" is a horrible strategy for incumbents to follow, resulting in a much poorer showing at the polls. For every 4 percent increase in the negativism of an incumbent's campaign, he or she drops 1 percent in the two-party vote. To phrase this result in a more upbeat way, incumbents who campaigned on their *own* accomplishments, abilities, and issue stands did significantly *better* at the polls than incumbents who chose instead to attack their opponents.[4]

This model shows no significant effect of a challenger's negativism on the outcome of the election, although this variable does have the predicted sign. If we ignore statistical significance, the model suggests that for every 9 percent increase in the negativism of a challenger's campaign, his or her share of the two-party vote increases by 1 percent.

Before moving on, we draw the reader's attention to an important comparison between the base model, which does not include estimates of the campaign's tone, and model 1, which does: an increase in the adjusted R^2 from .25 to .34. This increase is huge, and it clearly illustrates a point that is surprisingly difficult to make statistically, particularly with aggregate-level data: *The nature of the campaign matters*. It substantiates our claim that it is not just money, but *how* candidates choose to spend their campaign funds, that influences the outcome of the election.

The campaign tone variables in model 1 are simply the percentage of all statements from each candidate's campaign that attacked an opponent. Operationalizing the crucial independent variables in terms of raw percentages is straightforward and easy to understand, but it makes the implicit assumption that all candidates are equally able to get their messages across to the voters. At best, this is a dubious assumption. In reality, candidates with larger campaign war chests would be able to deliver their messages much more effectively. Thus model 2 employs *weighted* measures of campaign tone.[5] This weighting should magnify the effects of the campaign for candidates with a lot of money to spend, while minimizing the effects of the campaign among those with relatively few resources to help them disseminate their messages. The coefficients for the two weighted measures of campaign tone represent the *change* from the unweighted estimate for every one point increase in spending.[6]

To walk the reader through the results, model 2 estimates that when an incumbent has no money to spend, going negative helps (although not significantly). The .33 coefficient translates into a one point boost in the vote percentage for a three point increase in campaign negativism. The model estimates that campaign negativism is equally effective for challengers with no money to spend—and this time the estimate is statistically reliable.

But no incumbents have nothing to spend, and few challengers do. If we look at what the model predicts for mean levels of campaign spending, we see that the net effect of campaign negativism for incumbents is $-.26$,[7] a change that just misses conventional levels of statistical significance, while the net effect for challengers is greatly reduced to $-.11$, a change that is also nearly statistically significant. The model estimates that at high levels of spending, when the campaign is very intense, going negative hurts the chances of both incumbents and challengers.

These results hardly validate the presumed overwhelming effectiveness of negative campaigning. But we still may not have things right. The previous two models assumed that the effect of negative campaigning by either candidate was independent of the level of negative campaigning by his or her opponent. This assumption still seems unrealistic. Model 3 relaxes this assumption by including an even more elaborate interaction term, combining weighted incumbent negativism and weighted challenger negativism. By this final elaboration, we hope to capture the campaign interplay between incumbents and challengers. But, in the end, it does not improve our explanation because of the limitations of our data. Even ignoring significance levels, the magnitude of the estimated effect is so small as to be of no practical importance.[8]

Our initial findings, then, paint at best a very mixed picture of the usefulness of negative campaigning. Going negative would appear to be a very poor strategy for incumbents, although it could be a somewhat more effective strategy for challengers (or at least one that is not counterproductive).

We can push these results one more step. We may be distorting the picture by including all available elections in which the incumbent was seeking reelection. Westlye (1991) points to the competitiveness (or "intensity") of the election as an important influence on voters' decisions. Some incumbents are so popular, and some states are so dominated by one of the political parties, that the Senate election is never really in doubt. In such cases the campaign, whatever its nature, probably has little effect on the outcome of the election. If we limit our sample to competitive races, negative campaigning may prove to be a more effective strategy, particularly for incumbents.

Using *Congressional Quarterly*'s fall projections, we divided our elections into two groups—those where each candidate was judged to have at least some chance of winning and those that were largely noncompetitive (considered to be "safe" for one of the parties)—and repeated the analyses in these two groups. The results for the campaign tone variables are reported in table 4.2, separately for competitive and noncompetitive races. Contrary to the hypothesis, the findings do not show much of a difference between the two kinds of contests. Indeed, the case for the efficacy of negative campaigning becomes even weaker in competitive races.

Controlling on the competitiveness of the election thus makes negative campaigning appear to be an even less effective strategy than it did initially, at least when the campaign has a chance to affect the outcome of the election. One refinement does show a suggestive difference, however. When we break the overall measures of campaign negativism into separate measures of policy-based and person-based negativism, neither strategy appears to work for

Table 4.2   Percent Vote for Incumbent Senator, State Level, Controlling on Competitiveness of Election

75 Competitive Elections

	Model 1		Model 2		Model 3	
	B	S.E.	B	S.E.	B	S.E.
Incumbent Negativism	−.04	.08	.41	.30	−.03	.36
Challenger Negativism	−.01	.09	−.41**	.15	−.53**	.16
Incumbent Neg. × Spending			−.13	.09	.06	.13
Challenger Neg. × Spending			.16**	.05	.28**	.08
Weighted Inc. Negativism × Weighted Chal. Negativism					−.000@	.000

66 Noncompetitive Elections

	Model 1		Model 2		Model 3	
	B	S.E.	B	S.E.	B	S.E.
Incumbent Negativism	−.10	.06	−.41	.52	−.87@	.45
Challenger Negativism	−.13@	.08	−.12	.18	−.19	.13
Incumbent Neg. × Spending			.09	.14	.26@	.15
Challenger Neg. × Spending			−.01	.09	.10	.09
Weighted Inc. Negativism × Weighted Chal. Negativism					−.001@	.001

@p < .10**   p < .01
Note: All equations include the same variables as those shown in table 4.1. Weighted incumbent and challenger negativism are negativism multiplied by spending.

incumbents (as both coefficients, either by themselves or weighted by spending, have negative signs), but policy-based attacks by a challenger stand out as the only campaign strategy by either candidate to have its predicted effect. Although the effect is not quite statistically significant, the results do hint that policy-based attacks (but not personal attacks) by challengers could be efficacious. We will look more carefully at the separate effects of policy-based and personal attacks in the next section.[9]

Does It Work? Cross-Level Survey Analyses

For a more precise analysis, we now turn to individual-level survey data for the 109 Senate elections between 1992 and 2002 for which we have both aggregate and survey data. This is a cross-level analysis; while the survey data are measured at the individual level, the crucial campaign tone and spending variables are measured at the state level.

Table 4.3 presents the results of three increasingly complex models of vote for the incumbent senator. These analyses conceptually replicate models 1, 2, and 3 from the aggregate analysis, with individual-level measures replacing their aggregate-level equivalents whenever possible. The dependent variable, again, is vote for the incumbent. We continue to employ two-stage estimation procedures for candidate spending and campaign tone, using the same first-stage estimates employed earlier.

We focus on the campaign tone variables but note in passing that the aggregate- and individual-level analyses provide very similar results for the other variables in the equations, with the individual-level results generally proving somewhat stronger. For example, presidential popularity, measured at the national level, was only significant in the OLS estimates of the base model but is highly significant in all three variations (measured at the individual level) including the survey data. Both incumbent spending and challenger spending have significant effects on the outcome of the election, again equal in magnitude (but of course opposite in direction).

Turning to the campaign tone variables, the results of the individual-level analysis are strikingly similar to those from the aggregate analysis. Model 1 suggests that attacking the opponent hurts the incumbent a lot, and it helps the challenger only a small (and nonsignificant) amount. Weighting campaign tone by spending does not change the picture at all. While the raw, unweighted campaign tone measures have their predicted signs when spending is zero, the model quickly estimates incumbent negativism to become counterproductive, while the effect of challenger negativism approaches zero, as spending increases to the actual levels in these elections.

The most realistic model is certainly the last. Here we make two impor-

Table 4.3   Vote for Incumbent Senator, Individual Level, 1992–2002

	Model 1		Model 2		Model 3	
	B	S.E.	B	S.E.	B	S.E.
Constant	.99*	.43	−.85	1.26	−.86	1.19
Approve President's Job Perf.	.80***	.08	.80***	.08	.79***	.08
Midterm Election	.03	.13	.06	.14	.05	.14
National Economy Worse	.22*	.05	.24*	.11	.23*	.12
Change in PCDI	−.08	.05	−.07	.05	−.06	.05
Party Identification	1.50***	.10	1.51***	.10	1.52***	.10
Ideological Identification	.78***	.14	.80***	.14	.78***	.14
Policy Preferences	.74***	.16	.72***	.16	.73***	.16
Incumbent Scandal	−.26	.29	−.14	.31	−.12	.32
Incumbent Controversy	.59*	.29	.65*	.32	.63@	.34
Incumbent Health Problem	−.25	.83	−.22	.83	−.23	.83
Challenger a Governor	.16	.45	.29	.49	.29	.50
Challenger Major Office Holder	−.09	.24	−.09	.24	−.09	.25
Challenger in House	.50	.31	.50	.33	.49	.34
Challenger Minor Office Holder	.33@	.20	.27	.20	.27	.20
Incumbent Spending	.39**	.15	1.06**	.40	1.05**	.42
Challenger Spending	−.39	.15	−.45@	.24	−.47	.30
Incumbent Negativism	−2.17**	.70	3.06	3.00	2.73	3.21
Challenger Negativism	−.35	.96	−.67	1.61	−.75	1.83
Incumbent Negativism × Spending			−1.70@	.94	−1.49	1.14
Challenger Negativism × Spending			.05	.54	.11	.94
Weighted Incumbent Negativism × Weighted Challenger Negativism					−.05	.33
Campaign Exposure					.86*	.44
Exposure × Weighted Inc. Neg.					−.63**	.22
Exposure × Weighted Chal. Neg.					−.28	.26
Exposure × Weighted Inc. Neg. × Weighted Chal. Neg.					.91*	.38
Model Chi-Square	1480.69***		1484.02***		1496.40***	
Nagelkerke Pseudo R²	.56		.57		.57	
Percent Correctly Classified	82.7		82.3		83.1	

@p < .10*   p < .05   **p < .01   ***p < .001

Note: Table entries are two-stage logistic regression coefficients. Weighted incumbent and challenger negativism are negativism multiplied by spending. The equations also included dummy variables for election year, and individual level controls for age, education, income, race, and gender. N = 2,839.

tant additions to the model. First, as in the aggregate-level analysis, we allow the candidates' campaigns to interact with each other, thus removing the unrealistic assumption that the effect of a candidate's campaign is independent of what his or her opponent is doing. Second, we introduce an *individual-level* measure of campaign exposure, which allows us to do a much better job of discriminating between those more or less exposed to the campaign. As described in appendix B, we constructed such a measure by combining questions about individuals' general interest in the campaign and their attention to national news on television and in newspapers. We added this new variable, plus interactions between it and all of the crucial campaign variables.

The results, shown as model 3 in table 4.3, produce a number of significant effects, particularly the interactions with campaign exposure. Figure 4.1 helps illustrate what the model is telling us. When voter exposure to the campaign is high, shown in figure 4.1a, increasing negativism by incumbents significantly *decreases* their likely vote (or, more precisely, the probability of their winning a particular vote). Overall, incumbents who run relatively positive races will win 11 percent more votes than incumbents who run relatively negative campaigns. The effect of challenger negativism is almost nil, however, as illustrated by the three flat horizontal lines. Challengers are likely to receive only 1 percent more of the vote as their campaigns become more negative.

The picture changes only slightly when respondents have relatively low exposure to the campaign, as shown in figure 4.1b. The disadvantage that incumbents accrue for going negative reduces from 11 percent to only 7 or 8 percent, while negative campaigning is predicted to be slightly more effective for challengers. Thus nothing in the survey data changes the findings we have already sketched, a judgment of the futility and ineffectiveness of negative campaigning. It would appear to be a significantly counterproductive strategy for incumbents, and at best a mildly productive strategy for challengers.

We also considered the effects of the competitiveness of the elections by controlling for *Congressional Quarterly*'s fall projections, taking advantage of the greater sample size available from the survey data, to separately analyze three kinds of contests: noncompetitive races considered to be "safe" for one of the parties; those where one candidate (almost always the incumbent) was the clear favorite but there was at least some chance for an upset; and highly competitive races. No matter how we cut the data, however, the pattern of results does not change much from that presented in table 4.3. Controlling for the variables already in our analyses, the predicted competitiveness of the race explains no additional variance.

Neither did levels of partisanship. Prior research has shown that campaigns typically reinforce the bias of partisans rather than convince them to switch from one candidate to another. This same reasoning would lead us to expect that independents could be most open to persuasion from campaign messages—at least if they are exposed to them—as they have no partisan lens through which to view the campaign. Partisans may view campaigns in such a biased manner that the actual effectiveness of negative campaigning is obscured (or even reversed). According to this line of reasoning, the true effects of negative campaigning can be seen only among independents.

To test this hypothesis we ran model 3 again, separately for independents and partisans. There is simply no support for this hypothesis in our data.

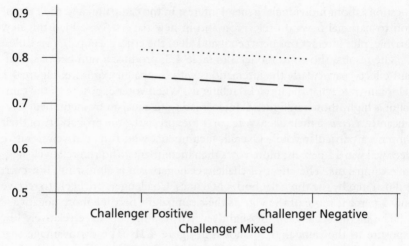

A. High Exposure to the Campaign

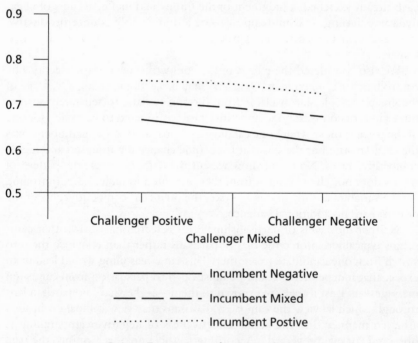

——————— Incumbent Negative

— — — - Incumbent Mixed

················· Incumbent Postive

B. Low Exposure to the Campaign

Figure 4.1   Net Effect of Campaign Negativism on Probability of Vote for Incumbent Senator, Individual Level

None of the campaign tone variables, either by themselves, weighted by spending, or combined with campaign exposure, were significantly related to the vote choice among independents. Political independence—even controlling for campaign exposure—*weakens* the apparent effect of the campaign. The results for partisans look much like those in table 4.3 for all voters.

Finally, we also distinguish between issue-based and person-based negativism with our different models.[10] Table 4.4 presents the results of a slightly reduced and simplified model. The pattern of results, although rarely achieving conventional levels of statistical significance, is nonetheless quite interesting and generally reinforces what we found in the aggregate analysis. Focusing on the four weighted campaign tone variables, and the interactions between them and campaign exposure, we see that issue-based negativism always has its intended effect, in that it helps the electoral chances of its practitioners, both incumbents and challengers, with the latter effect approaching statistical significance. But person-based negativism hurts both incumbents and challengers. This counterproductive effect of person-based negativism is exacerbated (at least for challengers) among respondents who pay a great deal of attention to the campaign. This is the only hint in our survey data (and admittedly, it is a weak one) that voters distinguish between issue-based and person-based attacks. Still the evidence, weak as it is, conforms with the hypothesis that voters find issue-based attacks more acceptable than person-based attacks (Kahn and Kenney 1999b). We will have more to say about this issue in the concluding chapter.

Implications

We started this project with some skepticism that negative political campaigning really helps the candidates who utilize it. Moreover, knowing the methodological difficulties facing any researcher trying to detect campaign or media effects of any stripe, we feared that our data would not be powerful enough to detect significant effects. But our results surprised us: Not only did they prove to be reasonably powerful, but we found at least some situations in which a challenger would be helped by attacking the opponent. Our basic findings were replicated across both aggregate- and individual-level data sets.

Still, our skepticism about the inordinate power of negative campaigning seems to have been justified, and our findings clearly should not be read as validating or encouraging negative campaigning, either normatively or empirically. A full accounting of the evidence suggests that, as often as not, attacking the opponent can be as dangerous in campaigns as throwing a boomerang in the wilderness. All else equal, our results suggest that incumbents almost always would have won more votes than they actually did had they run more positive campaigns. Challengers do not seem to be similarly hurt by going negative, but then neither are they helped very much by this strat-

Table 4.4   Effect of Issue- and Person-Based Negativism on Vote for Incumbent Senator, Individual Level, 1992–2002

	B	S.E.
Constant	.25	1.39
Approve President's Job Perf.	.81***	.08
Midterm Election	.17	.15
National Economy Worse	.25*	.12
Change in PCDI	−.09	.06
Party Identification	1.53***	.10
Ideological Identification	.80***	.14
Policy Preferences	.71***	.16
Incumbent Scandal	.04	.34
Incumbent Controversy	.72*	.35
Incumbent Health Problem	−.61	.85
Challenger a Governor	.97@	.60
Challenger Major Office Holder	.05	.27
Challenger in House	.92*	.42
Challenger Minor Office Holder	.22	.22
Incumbent Spending	.95*	.46
Challenger Spending	−.59@	.33
Incumbent Issue-Based Negativism	−5.95	7.92
Incumbent Person-Based Negativism	4.21	7.42
Challenger Issue-Based Negativism	1.88	2.74
Challenger Person-Based Negativism	−3.38	2.21
Incumbent Issue-Negativism × Spending	1.09	2.45
Incumbent Person-Negativism × Spending	−2.53	2.32
Challenger Issue-Negativism × Spending	−1.59@	.92
Challenger Person-Negativism × Spending	1.52@	.87
Campaign Exposure	.11	.32
Weighted Incumbent Issue-Negativism × Exposure	−.28	.31
Weighted Incumbent Person-Negativism × Exposure	−.27	.33
Weighted Challenger Issue-Negativism × Exposure	.03	.20
Weighted Challenger Person-Negativism × Exposure	.51*	.23
Model Chi-Square	1500.55***	
Nagelkerke Pseudo R²	.57	
Percent Correctly Classified	82.8	

@p < .10   *p < .05   ***p < .001
Note: Table entries are two-stage logistic regression coefficients. Weighted incumbent and challenger negativism are negativism multiplied by spending. The equations also included dummy variables for election year, and individual level controls for age, education, income, race, and gender. N = 2,839.

egy. Victory is still unlikely unless challengers both outspend and outattack their opponents—and few incumbents will give them this kind of free ride.

If political consultants were to ask our advice, would these results provide sufficient information to devise a successful Senate campaign? As noted earlier, we find no support for the conventional wisdom that negative campaigning is inordinately effective. Besides this general conclusion, however, our methodology is too crude to provide any detailed advice. We have only broad summaries of the strategies that were employed by the different candidates during the last months of the campaigns. Tracking more subtle shifts and variations in what a candidate does over time—and we know such variation exists (Roberts and Alvarez 1996)—is beyond what we can detect with our data.

Although the benefits of negative campaigning are relatively small, the costs could still be considerable, not simply in campaign dollars spent inefficiently (or even counterproductively), but in the more important effects on the dialogue of democracy. Negative campaigning has been associated with declining turnout and lower levels of political efficacy and trust in government. We will examine these more systemic effects in chapter 6. Normatively, while we do not join all the criticisms made, we too would object to negative campaigning that involves personal attacks unrelated to the governing capabilities of candidates or that distorts their records and issue positions. Nothing in our data suggests this sort of campaigning would be effective—but neither do our data suggest that it is very widespread, at least in campaigns involving incumbents. In the next chapter, we will consider races without incumbents, contests for open seats. We will then return to the effects of negative campaigning on the political system and, in the final chapter, to the normative issues raised by these tactics.

Notes

This chapter draws on material originally published as Richard R. Lau and Gerald M. Pomper, "Effectiveness of Negative Campaigning in U.S. Senate Elections," *American Journal of Political Science* 46 (January 2002): 47–66.

1. These are all indicators of less efficient estimation. This results in much less statistical power to detect significant effects, as seen in the absence of statistically significant effects of any of the control variables in the 2SLS base model. The standard errors *least* affected by 2SLS estimation (but the coefficients *most* affected by the change) are those associated with the two problematic spending variables, the only actual difference between the two models.

2. The lack of impact is shown by the size of the standard error, which exceeds the regression coefficient (B). A coefficient must be about twice as large as its standard error to achieve conventional levels of statistical significance.

3. This is the category excluded from the list of challenger dummy variables.

4. Since every statement is coded as either positive or negative, the percent negativism of a campaign equals 100 minus the percent positivism. Thus if we had created a measure of the relative *positivism* of the two major-party campaigns, the −.25 coefficient would simply reverse to +.25. As one early reader of this manuscript pointed out to us, the interpretation of the marginal effectiveness (or ineffectiveness) of negative campaigning presented in the text is based crucially

on our model of candidate decision making. If candidates know precisely how effective different campaign strategies will be in their specific states, and choose accordingly, then our results reflect the relatively greater number of races where going negative is the best strategy for challengers to follow, whereas staying positive is the better strategy for the large majority of incumbents, and it would be wrong to present our results as if *all* incumbents would do 1 percent worse at the polls with 4 percent more negative campaigning, and so on. We suspect, however, that ambiguity and uncertainty, rather than precision, characterize the world of campaign decision making. The basic question comes down to whether there is a *single* distribution of campaign effects that includes all campaigns, or if instead there are two (or more) distributions of campaign effects, one where negative campaigning is more effective, another where positive campaigning is more effective, and candidates know which distribution they are in. Our intuition tells us that, even if there are multiple distributions of campaign effects, there is so much overlap between them that for all practical purposes, they might as well be considered a single distribution. The argument for uncertainty and a single distribution of campaign effects is particularly strong for model 3, where all campaign effects are conditional on what the opponent does, and all campaign decisions must be made (at least in the short run) without precise knowledge of how the opponent is going to respond.

5. The weighting is calculated by multiplying the same raw percentages used in model 1 by the campaign spending variable (the logarithm of spending per capita).

6. Operationalizing the crucial independent variables in this manner makes greater intuitive sense, but it also makes the results more difficult to understand. Now there are two variables representing each campaign's tone, the raw (unweighted) estimates and the new weighted measures. The correct interpretation for the two unweighted variables is that they represent the effects of campaign negativism when each candidate has no money to spend on campaigning (a situation that never occurs for incumbents, and almost never occurs for challengers). The interpretation of the two candidate spending variables—our weights—would also change. Now they would estimate the effect of campaign spending when the candidate's campaign was totally positive.

7. For incumbents, the net effect is calculated by taking the unweighted coefficient for campaign tone and adding to it the product of the coefficient for weighted campaign tone multiplied by the mean spending level (3.5). Algebraically: $.33 + (-.17 \cdot 3.5) = -.26$. The same process is employed for the effect on challengers, whose mean spending equals 2.1. Algebraically: $-.32 + (.10 \cdot 2.1) = -.11$.

8. Including such an interaction term in the model is asking an awful lot of our data, for two reasons. First, we have only 141 cases, and interaction terms tend to be relatively inefficient. And second, as seen in chapter 3, the incumbent and the challenger tend to match each other in campaign negativism, so we have a lot of cases where both candidates are relatively negative or both stay relatively

positive but very few cases where one candidate is positive but the opponent is negative. It should not be surprising, then, that this interaction term fails to approach statistical significance.

9. Before moving on, we should mention several additional analyses that are not reported in table 4.1. We followed the guidelines of Abramowitz (1988) and Gerber (1998) in creating a dummy variable for a "celebrity" challenger, but this variable always had the wrong sign and never approached statistical significance. We also created a measure of the "issue proximity" of the incumbent to the mean ideology of that state's electorate, but this measure had no effect whatsoever in any analysis.

10. This is asking a lot of the data, for the number of campaign tone variables, and thus the number of crucial interaction terms, doubles. The data are not quite up to the task, and when we examined the equivalent of model 3 from table 4.3, none of the crucial campaign variables or their interactions were significant. The reduced model in table 4.4 includes none of the four possible interaction terms between the two indicators of the incumbent's campaign tone and the two indicators of the challenger's campaign tone.

Negative Campaigning in Open-Seat Contests

5

C ONTESTS FOR SENATE SEATS usually include an incumbent seeking reelection to the prestigious and powerful chamber. In about a quarter of the races during the six election years we are considering, however, the seat was open, with both the Republican and Democratic candidates new entrants into the competition. In this chapter, we analyze the effectiveness of negative campaigning in this distinctive set of elections, using methods similar to those employed in the previous chapter, the analysis of incumbent candidates.

Negative campaigning helped Republican James Inhofe overcome the early lead of Democrat Dave McCurdy in the Oklahoma Senate contest of 1994. Inhofe relied on negative campaigning, according to press reports. The Republican's negative tactics were emphasized in five out of six press reports of his campaign, in sharp contrast to the negativity emphasis in only three of ten reports of McCurdy's campaign. Inhofe described his successful campaign strategy (Burger 1994):

> "The Three Gs" will put him over the top in overwhelmingly Democratic McCurtain County, Rep. Jim Inhofe tells a small group in a back room of the Ideal Restaurant here. . . . "God, gays, and guns."
>
> Specifically, Inhofe attacks McCurdy—on paper, on the airwaves, and in personal campaign appearances—for the Democrat's May 1993 vote to pass President Clinton's first budget, his vote for the assault weapons ban that was included in the crime bill, and his support for allowing gays in the military. . . .
>
> On Monday, Inhofe began airing an ad depicting McCurdy as Pinocchio, complete with visuals of McCurdy's nose growing as, the ad asserts, he lies about his work. . . .
>
> On the campaign trail, Inhofe himself highlights [his own] conservative views.
>
> During a brief question period in the Ideal Restaurant, for example, one of the guests asks, "The theory of evolution is taught in our high school. What's the difference between teaching that and teaching the Bible?"

"I don't see any difference," Inhofe says.

Meanwhile, Inhofe pounds the gun issue.

In Nowata, for example, Inhofe works the Bliss Restaurant's lunch counter.

"Let me give you this, since you've got a camouflage jacket on," Inhofe says to a customer, handing him a sheet touting his endorsement from the National Rifle Association.

In the office of the Pawhuska Police Department, Inhofe says to one man sitting on a desk, "You ever shoot a gun?"

"Sure."

"Well, then you want to read that," Inhofe says, handing him an NRA handout.

"What about deer hunting?" someone else asks.

"There won't be much deer hunting if you leave McCurdy in. There won't be any guns to shoot 'em with."

Stopping at a small, roadside barbecue restaurant in Pawhuska, Inhofe says to Charlie Chambers, a cowboy hat–wearing man entering the establishment, "Lemme give you some gun stuff."

"We pack a gun," Chambers says.

"You won't be able to much longer if you get McCurdy," Inhofe says.

Attention and electoral success, however, do not necessarily depend on negative campaigning. In an open-seat race two years later in Maine, Susan Collins also won a Senate seat for the Republicans. She succeeded with a campaign that was less negative than that of her Democratic opponent, Joseph Brennan, and actually conducted one of the least negative campaigns in our data set. The differences in the campaigns are apparent in reports on the issue of gun control (Higgins 1996):

The two front-runners in the race for the U.S. Senate displayed distinctively divergent styles Thursday as the campaign wound down to its last six days.

Bangor Republican Susan M. Collins boarded her "Collins Express" tour bus to visit several northern and eastern Maine towns while Portland Democrat Joseph E. Brennan hosted anti-gun activist Sarah Brady only days before deer season. Brady toured the Lyseth School in Portland and used the opportunity to formally endorse Brennan for pledging to oppose any efforts to repeal the ban on assault weapons. . . .

Collins, who began her tour of Houlton at 7:30 a.m. and wound up in Bangor at 4 p.m., observed that most Maine residents must wonder why Brady is making such a fuss over semi-automatic firearms.

"Those weapons are not only not a problem in Maine, they're not a problem nationwide, when you look at the crime statistics," she said. "If you really believe that banning guns is the way to reduce crime—which I don't think is the answer, but Joe appears to—then he should be for banning handguns because they're involved in 55 percent of all homicides and the so-called assault weapons are involved in less than one half of one percent." . . .

Bob Tyrer, Collins' campaign manager, said that Brady's statements regarding the GOP candidate constituted "an offensive attack" on his boss's integrity, adding that Brennan had received thousands of dollars from anti-gun groups.

"Yet, we do not suggest that his anti-gun views are a result of those donations," he said.

While Brennan toured schools Thursday in Saco and Portland with Brady, Collins was on the road visiting Lincoln, Millinocket and Dover-Foxcroft. It was a strategy she used at the end of her 1994 gubernatorial campaign. This time, though, she enjoyed a smoother ride and bigger reception.

"There are larger and more enthusiastic crowds everywhere I go," she said. "Today when I was campaigning, I shook hundreds of hands.

There wasn't a single person who didn't say that he or she wasn't voting for me. It was wonderful."

Analyzing Open-Seat Contests

Open-seat candidates face special problems in winning elections. Like challengers, they are less familiar to the voters and must work harder than incumbents to gain recognition and support. Because they are less prominent, they have probably had fewer opportunities to establish networks among interest groups and contributors. These factors might be expected to lead open-seat candidates to use negative campaigning more than incumbents and perhaps to be particularly dependent on the tactic in winning elections. As we have already seen in chapter 3 (see table 3.1 and figure 3.2), this is indeed the case. The campaigns of candidates for open seats are about 10 percent more negative than are the campaigns of incumbents running for reelection. This figure is slightly (and indistinguishably) less than the average for challengers.

But an open-seat candidate is also different from the typical challenger. A strong candidate from the opposition party may choose to sit out an election rather than challenge a popular incumbent, but that same candidate would jump into the election if the seat were open. This means that candidates for open seats are usually more experienced and better known than the typical challenger. In our data almost half of the challengers (46 percent) had no previous electoral experience; this was true of less than a quarter (22 percent) of the open-seat candidates. At the other end of the political experience spectrum, 5 of the 153 challengers in our data set were former or sitting governors, compared with 11 of the 100 open-seat candidates.

Of course the incentives are the same for candidates from each party, which means that the candidates for open-seat races are typically much more evenly matched in terms of prior political experience than is usually the case when an incumbent faces a challenger. This translates into open-seat races being much more competitive than the typical election when an incumbent is seeking reelection. In the 1992 to 2002 period, the average margin of victory when incumbents were seeking reelection was more than 23 percent—and this includes all of the elections where the incumbent lost! The average margin of victory in the fifty open-seat contests was almost half that—almost exactly 12 percent. All of these factors make it particularly tempting to try to shape public perceptions to disadvantage the opponent. It is also possible, however, that negative campaigning can disproportionately damage an open-seat candidate, who may gain an unwanted bad reputation by using the practice. We will soon see that negativism can be a two-edged sword for those who use this weapon.

The analysis of open-seat races brings both new challenges and new opportunities. The challenges are of two kinds. First, there are simply fewer open-seat contests to study, compared with elections where an incumbent is seeking reelection. From 1992 to 2002, there were 158 contests where an incumbent was seeking reelection and only 50 open-seat contests. (We have campaign data from 49 of those elections.) We have survey data available from 1,070 respondents and 37 of those elections, compared with more than 2,800 respondents and 109 incumbent versus challenger contests. This means we will face "degrees of freedom" problems, particularly in the aggregate analysis, where each case is a separate election. With the conventional rule of thumb that one should have at least five observations for every predictor in a regression, we are limited in what we can do.

The second problem is related to the first. There is simply a dearth of research on open-seat Senate contests. Abramowitz and Segal (1992) consider them explicitly (if quite briefly); Kahn and Kenney (1999b), Krasno (1994), and Westyle (1991) do not. Abramowitz and Segal (1992) included seven predictors in their aggregate-level model of open-seat Senate elections between 1974 and 1986: measures of state-level partisanship and ideology, a dummy variable indicating a midterm election, survey-based measures of presidential popularity and national party competence,[1] and measures of relative candidate experience and relative candidate spending. They found only the last two candidate-based variables had significant effects on the outcome of open-seat contests.

This relative paucity of research leaves us much more to our own devices in designing the analysis. That gives us a good opportunity to contribute to the literature on Senate elections beyond examining the effects of campaign tone. But we also lack the comfort of comparing our results with previous findings that might assure us that we are doing things right.

Aggregate-Level Analysis

We started our analysis by reproducing Abramowitz and Segal's analysis. In appendix B, we describe measures of state partisanship and ideology, mid-term elections, and presidential popularity. For this chapter, we developed measures to compare the two major-party candidates in regard to two factors: spending and candidate quality or experience.

Spending is simply measured by dividing the Republican candidate's spending per capita by the sum of the Republican and Democrat's spending per capita. In regard to *candidate experience or quality*, we applied the same indicators used in the previous chapter to measure the quality of the challenger to each of the open-seat candidates. We created a single indicator of the quality of each candidate, and then combined them to create an indicator of relative candidate experience.[2] The limited number of cases available requires us (and Abramowitz and Segal before us) to combine separate measures of Democratic and Republican spending, and separate indicators of candidate quality, into the two relative measures already described.

We could not find comparable measures of party competence for all of the years in our data, and since it was not significant in Abramowitz and Segal's analysis, we did not try to develop close alternatives. Instead, we added a simple indicator of the party of the retiring senator who previously held the seat being contested, with the idea that it best represents partisan contexts, otherwise unmeasured, unique to each state.

The first two columns of table 5.1 show the results of this base model. The way we have coded the data, all coefficients should have a positive sign except the dummy variable for a midterm election, which should be negative. Three variables prove to be significant predictors in this base model: state ideology, the party of the retiring incumbent, and relative candidate spending. All else equal, the candidate from the party of the retiring incumbent does about five points better than his or her opponent in open-seat contests. For every three or four points that the percentage of conservatives in a state exceeds the percentage of liberals, the Republican candidate does about one point better in the election. And for every six points that the Republican share of two-party spending exceeds the Democratic share, the Republican candidate receives about one more percent of the two-party vote. In subsequent

Table 5.1   Effect of Negative Campaigning on Percent Republican Vote in Open-Seat Races for the U.S. Senate, State Level, 1992–2002

	Base Model		Model 1		Model 2	
	B	S.E.	B	S.E.	B	S.E.
State Partisanship	.02	.09	.05	.08	.08*	.03
State Ideology	.28*	.14	.28*	.13	.28***	.04
Party of Retiring Incumbent	5.06*	2.23	6.43**	2.10	6.46**	.70
Midterm Election	−2.48	2.00	−3.76*	1.84	−4.02***	.62
Presidential Popularity	−.03	.11	.08	.12	.18***	.04
Relative Candidate Experience	.72	.76	.41	.68	−.38	.24
Relative Candidate Spending	.17@	.09	.17*	.08	.17***	.03
Democratic Negativism			.17	.14	−.91***	.14
Republican Negativism			.15	.11	.84***	.12
Weighted Democratic Negativism					.75***	.10
Weighted Republican Negativism					−.40***	.08
Constant	35.51***	5.32	34.86***	4.66	34.69***	.55
Adjusted R²	.30		.36		.56	
Standard Error	6.09		5.81		4.81	

@ p < .10*   p < .05   ***p < .01   ***p < .001
Note: Table entries are 2SLS estimates. N = 49.

models both presidential popularity and the midterm dummy variable become significant, indicating that open-seat races also partially reflect national forces. Unlike Abramowitz and Segal, however, in our last model state partisanship levels become significant, while our measure of relative candidate experience is never significant.[3]

We are much more interested in models 1 and 2, which add measures of the tone of each candidate's campaign. If attacking the opponent is an effective strategy to use in open-seat races, then the measure of the tone of the Democratic candidate's campaign should be negative, while the coefficient for the tone of the Republican's campaign should be positive. Model 1 simply adds indicators of the percentage of each candidate's campaign that was negative. Neither variable is statistically significant, although both exceed their standard error. Both coefficients are positive, indicating that going negative could be slightly effective for Republicans but slightly counterproductive for Democrats.[4]

Model 2 is more realistic, adding measures of the tone of each candidate's campaign weighted by their spending. Now we see a familiar pattern of results. While going negative seems to be an effective strategy for both Democrats and Republicans with no money, that strategy becomes increasingly counterproductive the more money candidates have to get their message across to voters. All four of the measures of campaign tone in model 2 are significant, although the backlash that Democrats experience with more campaign resources is almost twice that of what Republicans experience. The net effect suggests that going negative is somewhat more rewarding for Republican candidates.

Figure 5.1 illustrates these results. The figure illustrates the predicted marginal effect of campaign resources and campaign tone on the Republican percentage of the two-party vote, controlling on the other variables in the equation. Numbers above zero are a net advantage to the Republican; numbers below zero, a net advantage to the Democrat. Figure 5.1a shows what happens when the Democrat has a lot more money than the Republican. In such instances, the Democrats are always better off the more positive their campaigns (the dotted line is lower than the dashed line which is lower than the solid line), but Republicans are always better off the more negative their campaigns (all three lines slope upward).

When the Republican has a lot more campaign resources, however (shown in figure 5.1b), the situation reverses. Now Democrats are predicted to be better off the more negative their campaigns (the solid line is below the dashed line which is below the dotted line), while the tone of Republicans' campaigns are not predicted to matter much (the three lines are pretty flat). Put these two together—or look at situations where campaign resources are more equitably distributed—and Republican candidates are almost always predicted to do a little bit better the more negative their campaigns. For Democrats, on the other hand, the effectiveness of attacking their opponents is predicted to be much more contingent on relative finances. When they have more money than their opponents, it hurts them; when they have less money than their opponents, it generally helps them.

Cross-Level Survey Analysis

We tried to conceptually replicate this analysis with our survey data, replacing our state-level measures of partisanship and ideology, and the national-level measure of presidential popularity, with individual-level survey items. We also took advantage of the larger sample size available in the survey data to include separate measures of candidate experience and spending for the Democrat and the Republican. Once again all variables should be positively signed except for the dummy variable indicating a midterm election and the various spending and campaign tone measures for the Democrat, all of which should have negative signs.

The results are shown in table 5.2. Neither the simple nor the weighted measures of campaign tone prove to be significant in models 1 and 2. Only in model 3, which includes an interaction term between the weighted tone of the Democrat's and the Republican's campaigns, plus interactions of all the weighted campaign tone variables with an individual-level measure of campaign exposure, do we get any payoff from including measures of cam-

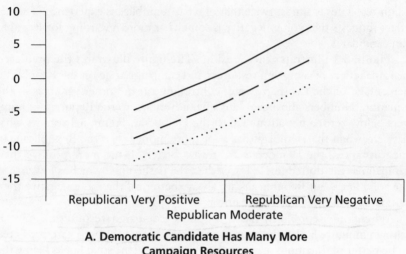

A. Democratic Candidate Has Many More Campaign Resources

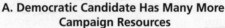

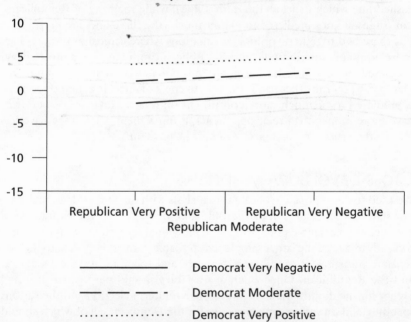

B. Republican Candidate Has Many More Campaign Resources

Figure 5.1   Net Effect of Campaign Tone on Percent Republican Vote in Open-Seat Senate Elections, Aggregate Level, Unequal Campaign Resources

Table 5.2   Effect of Negative Campaigning on Probability of Republican Vote in Open-Seat Races for the U.S. Senate, Individual Level, 1992–2002

	Model 1		Model 2		Model 3	
	B	S.E.	B	S.E.	B	S.E.
Constant	.81	.59	.77	.59	.78	.60
Approve President's Job Perf.	.51***	.07	.51***	.07	.52***	.07
Midterm Election	−1.14**	.46	−1.16*	.48	−.85@	.51
National Economy Worse	.05	.11	.05	.11	.04	.11
Change in PCDI	−.18@	.11	−.20@	.12	−.19	.12
Party Identification	.52***	.06	.52***	.06	.54***	.06
Ideological Identification	.24**	.08	.23**	.08	.22**	.08
Policy Preferences	.29	.31	.29	.32	.35	.31
Democrat Candidate Experience	−.16	.13	−.14	.15	−.19	.16
Republican Candidate Experience	.22@	.13	.25@	.14	.23	.15
Democrat Spending	−.70**	.27	−.72*	.30	−.61*	.31
Republican Spending	.56*	.27	.59*	.28	.51@	.28
Democrat Negativism	−.02	.02	−.02	.05	.02	.06
Republican Negativism	−.03	.02	.02	.05	.04	.05
Weighted Democratic Negativism			.00	.04	−.04	.05
Weighted Republican Negativism			−.03	.03	−.05	.03
Weighted Democratic Negativism × Weighted Republican Negativism					−.002*	.001
Campaign Exposure					−.28**	.10
Exposure × Weighted Dem. Neg.					.02	.01
Exposure × Weighted Rep. Neg.					.00	.01
Exposure × Weighted Dem. Neg. × Weighted Rep. Neg.					.001	.001
Model Chi-Square	629.48***		630.62***		642.60***	
Nagelkerke Pseudo R²	.61		.61		.62	
Percent Correctly Classified	83.4		83.5		82.6	

@p < .10   *p < .05   **p < .01   ***p < .001

Note: Table entries are two-stage logistic regression coefficients. Weighted Democratic and Republican negativism are negativism multiplied by spending. The equations also included dummy variables for election year, and individual level controls for age, education, income, race, and gender. N = 1,070.

paign tone. The interaction term between the nature of the two candidates' campaigns is significant and negative. This suggests that attacking the opponent becomes a more and more counterproductive strategy for Republicans, the more their opponents attack them, but an increasingly successful strategy for Democrats, the more their opponents attack them.

Figure 5.2 helps illustrate these results, in two different contexts. Figure 5.2a shows what the model predicts when the Republican candidate has a two-to-one advantage over the Democrat in campaign resources. Republicans are predicted to do best (winning about 58 percent of the votes) when they keep their campaigns positive, irrespective of how the Democrats cam-

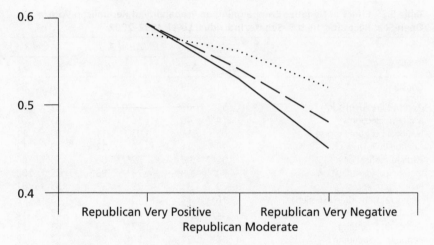

A. Republican Candidate Has More Campaign Resources

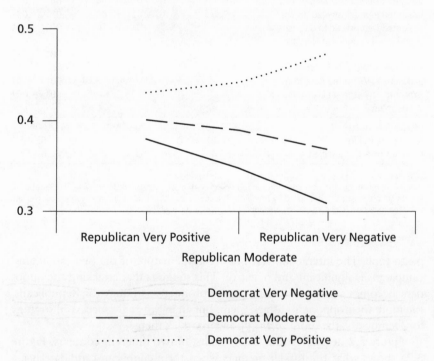

Democrat Very Negative
Democrat Moderate
Democrat Very Positive

B. Democratic Candidate Has More Campaign Resources

Figure 5.2   Effect of Campaign Tone on Probability of Republican Vote in Open-Seat Senate Elections, Individual Level, Relatively Equal Campaign Resources

paign. The Republican is still predicted to win when the campaign has moderate levels of negativism, although now the Democrat does a little better, the more he or she attacks the opponent. Only when the Republican runs a very negative campaign, however, does the Democrat have any chance of winning, and then only if he or she runs a moderately (or very) negative campaign—presumably responding to the attacks of the Republican with his or her own attacks.

Figure 5.2b illustrates what is predicted to happen when the Democrat has a two-to-one resource advantage. In such situations the Democrat is always predicted to win. But the Democrat is predicted to do better the more negative his or her campaign (the solid line is the lowest in the figure); the more negative the Republican's campaign, the better the Democrat is predicted to do, indicated by the line sloping down.

Implications

The data presented here are the first we have seen where measures of the candidates' campaigns have been included in an analysis of open-seat Senate elections. Indeed, there is so little analysis of open-seat Senate races that we should discuss our results more generally, quite apart from the campaigns themselves. Strong evidence suggests that open-seat races are, in part, a function of national forces. To begin with, both our aggregate and survey analyses indicate that popular presidents help open-seat candidates from their party a bit. This was also true for races where an incumbent was running for reelection, and the magnitude of the effect was comparably small in either case. But we also found consistent evidence that the president's party tends to *lose* open-seat *midterm* Senate races, and we saw no similar tendency for incumbent reelection races. We estimate such candidates do about 4 percent worse in the polls—a pretty significant hurdle in an open-seat race.

Open-seat contests provide a flexibility for the nation's politics that is less evident in incumbent races. In about a third of these contests, the Senate seat changed party hands, far more than the scarce defeats of 13 percent of incumbents (see table 1.1). Republicans were particularly successful in open-seat contests, and these races alone explain changes in party control of the upper chamber from 1992 to 2002.

When no incumbent is running, national political forces are more likely to have an effect, promoting greater responsiveness to the winds of public opinion. The election results are now affected by presidential popularity, the expected waning of that popularity in midterm elections (Campbell 1966), and national party loyalty. Incumbents are able to divert these winds, using the local advantages of spending, reputation, and constituent services. Their success can make politics rigid and senators nonresponsive. Their passings provide new, and necessary, opportunities for the fresh air of competitive politics.

.   But local factors are also clearly important in open-seat races. Conservative states tend to prefer Republican open-seat candidates, while more liberal states tend to favor Democrats. If anything, this preference is more symbolic than issue-based, however, as preference for more or less government spending had no significant impact in our survey analysis, controlling for liberal–conservative identification. The party of the retiring senator also mattered, and voters seem to prefer an open-seat candidate from that same party.

We found very limited evidence that candidate experience or quality mattered, however, controlling for the other variables in our equations. Although the single indicator of relative candidate experience, employed in the aggregate-level analysis, or the two distinct measures of candidate experience, employed in the survey analysis, almost always had the right sign and usually were larger than their standard error, the measures were rarely statistically significant, and then only at the one-tailed level. The problem, as already discussed, is that even across six election years there are relatively few open-seat cases to consider. Few cases translate into relatively limited variance and thus have little power to detect significant differences. At most, according to our analyses, the strongest possible candidate from one party (an ex-governor) facing the weakest possible candidate from the other party (one with no previous electoral experience) would enjoy a two- to three-point advantage at the polls—nothing to be sneered at but too little by itself to insure victory.

Turning to campaign factors, spending clearly matters—and by our estimates perhaps slightly more for the Democrat than the Republican. But we also found clear evidence that the nature of the campaign run by the candidates also mattered. In the aggregate analysis, the explainable variance indicated by our models increased from .30 to .56 as measures of campaign tone were added. That said, the pattern of results was complicated and often contradictory. Generally speaking, attacking the opponent seemed to be an increasingly counterproductive strategy the more money a candidate had to get his or her message across to voters. The aggregate-level results seem to suggest that going negative was a more effective strategy for Republicans than for Democrats to employ, while the survey analysis suggested just the opposite pattern, an inconsistency we suspect is due in large part to the limited number of cases available for study.

In no case, however, do our results provide a ringing endorsement for the effectiveness of attacking the opponent as a campaign strategy in open-seat elections. As we have found fairly consistently, negative campaigning is more of a specter than a real threat. In the previous chapter, we concluded that the practice did not help candidates consistently, and it actually can be harmful to some, particularly incumbents. Now we find similar limited impact in open-seat contests. Rational, victory-seeking candidates therefore have no *necessary* reason to adopt the practice. To do so, they must use their *judgment*, adopting their tactics to their particular campaign environment and accepting risks as well as opportunities.

In a larger sense, the fate of any individual candidate matters little, either to us as analysts or to the nation, which can sustain a fairly large number of naysayers and scoundrels. The more serious effects of negative campaigning may emerge in possible damaging effects on the political system. In the following chapter, we change our focus from the *intended* consequences of negative campaigning—winning votes for the candidates who utilize it—to its *unintended* but potentially quite serious overall consequences. We will now consider the effects of negative campaigning on voters' turnout, their perceptions of political efficacy, and their generalized trust in government.

Notes

1. This measure was based on a difference between the percentage of people thinking either party was better able to handle what they perceived to be the biggest problem facing the country, as reported in the last Gallup survey before the election.

2. We created a single indicator of the quality of each candidate: zero for a candidate with no electoral experience; 1 if the candidate held some relatively minor elected office; 2 if the candidate had been a member of the House of Representatives, was the mayor of a major city, or held some statewide office other than governor; and 3 for past governors of the state (or previous U.S. senators, as was the case in New Jersey in 2002 when Senator Bob Torricelli was forced to resign because of a fund-raising scandal, and former Senator Frank Lautenberg replaced him on the ballot for the now open Senate seat). We then subtracted the measure of the quality of the Democratic candidate from the comparable measure of the quality of the Republican.

3. We could speculate that incumbents anticipating retirement might help "groom" particularly strong replacement candidates. If this was true, then our indicator of the party of the retiring incumbent would partially represent relative candidate quality. Removing the former measure from the equations does not make relative candidate experience any stronger, however.

4. Notice once again, however, that adding measures of the campaign's tone noticeably increases the predictive power of the equation, as the adjusted R^2 increases from .30 to .36, and the standard error of the estimate decreases from 6.1 to 5.8.

Effects of Negative Campaigning on the Political System

THE CONVENTIONAL WISDOM is that negative campaigning decreases voter attachment to politics, resulting in voter withdrawal from politics, and particularly in lower turnout at the polls. To some observers (Morrison 1998), that effect could be seen in Nevada senator Harry Reid's reelection in 1998:

> The Overton woman in her 70s was almost embarrassed to admit it: For the first time in her life, this year she didn't vote.
>
> And she's laying the blame on TV political ads.
>
> She didn't give her name, but she was disgusted with the Republican and Democratic candidates, whose deceitful ads left her unwilling to go to the polls.
>
> Lower than predicted turnout in Nevada—49 percent instead of the projected 60 percent—suggests that ads may have kept other Nevadans at home this year as well. "The prediction of the secretary of state was higher than the turnout and that's a strong indicator those negative ads did have an effect," said Tim Fackler, UNLV assistant professor of political science.
>
> "I'm surprised by how many people are turned off by fairly mild attacks; they don't wish to see candidates attacking each other," Fackler said. "The negative ads work in a couple of ways. The most insidious is that they discourage participation."

In another race in 1998, however, the reelection of Russell Feingold in Wisconsin, the effects of negative campaigning were less obvious to observers (Timmerman 1998):

> Predictions on voter turnout were mixed. Some experts were saying voter turnout would be high today, while others were more pessimistic.
>
> But experts agreed that this year's intense negative campaigning and how it shapes voter attitudes is enormously complex and will be studied for years to come.
>
> "Right now, all bets are off," Virginia Sapiro, a University of

Wisconsin professor of political science who specializes in public opinion, said. . . .

The bombardment of television advertising, particularly nega-tive ads, could convince as many as 10 to 12 percent of those likely to vote to stay home, said Dennis Dresang, a UW political science professor.

On the other hand, Dresang and Sapiro agreed that the extreme closeness of the congressional races could crank the numbers up. . . .

Mobilization may also play a major role in close races, said UW political science professor Charles Franklin. The close races may produce a barrage of phone calls and voter drives, and may be enough to swing the election either way, he said.

Still, most experts say the stifling effect of negative ads will have significant influence on several races.

"I think it's going to have a downward effect," Dresang said of the negative ads. "I mean, I have friends that are political junkies and they're switching channels because of it."

The Uncertain Effects of Negative Campaigning

To observers of these two races, the effect of negative campaigning was clear in the first but very uncertain in the second. Scholarship paints a similarly murky picture. Ansolabehere, Iyengar, Simon, and Valentino (1994) were the first social scientists to provide serious evidence that the increase in nega-tive campaigning might harm the American political system (see also Ansola-behere and Iyengar 1995). In a series of clever and very realistic experiments conducted during statewide California elections, Ansolabehere and col-leagues found that subjects who viewed a single political attack (i.e., negative) ad during a local news broadcast were about 5 percent less likely to say they intend to vote in the upcoming election, compared with subjects who had seen a single advocacy (i.e., positive) ad during that same news broadcast. This effect was particularly pronounced among independents, who might be expected to be most receptive to persuasion by campaign messages.

These same researchers went on to examine newspaper articles about thirty-three U.S. Senate election campaigns in 1992, categorizing each of them as mostly positive, mixed, or mostly negative. Paralleling their experi-mental results, they found that actual turnout in the mostly negative races was almost 5 percent lower than turnout in the mostly positive campaigns, after controlling on a number of factors that typically predict turnout. Negative campaigning, it would seem, can have a significant demobilizing effect in elections.

This provocative finding did not long go unchallenged. Bartels (1996) found fault with the experimental analyses, Luskin and Bratcher (1994) challenged aspects of the aggregate turnout data in the 1992 U.S. Senate elections, and Finkel and Geer (1998) offered several theoretical reasons why negative campaigning might actually *increase* turnout. Most recently Kahn and Kenney (1999a), using survey data from the 1990 NES Senate election study, concluded that the tone of the political advertisements and the tone of newspaper coverage of the campaign both had positive (i.e., mobilizing)—though not statistically significant—effects on turnout. However, "mudslinging," as judged by the campaign managers of these Senate campaigns, did have a negative (i.e., demobilizing)—and significant—effect on turnout. Reviewing the cumulative evidence, as we did in chapter 2, there are about as many mobilizing as demobilizing effects in the literature.

We enter the fray with what we believe to be the most comprehensive data yet to address this question. With our aggregate state-level and our survey-based individual-level data sets, we here ask a very simple question: Can we find any evidence that the tone of a Senate election campaign has any significant effect (one way or the other) on turnout? We then go on to look at other potential effects on the political system.

We begin with a very basic hypothesis, that negative campaigning will influence turnout. We refine this general hypothesis in several ways. We would not expect a negative campaign to affect citizens who are barely exposed to it, so we extend this initial hypothesis with several methods aimed at measuring differential exposure to the campaign. We then follow up the suggestion (Ansolabehere et al. 1994) that the demobilizing effects of negative campaigns might be particularly strong among political independents. We will test this hypothesis indirectly with our aggregate data and much more directly with our survey data.

We further examine the recent report (Kahn and Kenney 1999a) that the tone of the campaign newspaper coverage had a positive effect on turnout but that mudslinging, as judged by campaign consultants, had a negative effect. We do not have data from campaign consultants, but we can attempt to approximate judgments of mudslinging in two different ways. First, it is possible that such judgments are made when there are a lot of *personal* attacks (as opposed to *issue*-based attacks) on the opponent. If so, then our separate measures of issue-based and person-based negativism may be able to pick up this distinction. Alternatively, it is possible that judgments of mudslinging tend to be made only at extremely high levels of overall negativism. We will consider curvilinear effects to explore this possibility.

Examining the Effects in States: Aggregate Data

To examine the effects of negative campaigning, we will employ both of our data sets, beginning with the aggregate data on elections and then the survey data on individual voters.

According to the demobilization hypothesis, as the tone of a campaign becomes more negative (i.e., as both candidates engage in more negative campaigning), it becomes more likely that people will be turned off by politics and less likely that they will vote. In table 6.1, we use the aggregate data, where each senatorial election is one case of the total 191 in the time period. Turnout in each Senate election is regressed on a series of predictors that have been associated with turnout (see Jackson 1997 and Timpone 1998 for recent state-level analyses of turnout), along with dummy variables representing election year. In the basic formulation, model 1, we find that turnout is significantly higher (carrying a positive sign) in presidential election years, in

Table 6.1   State-Level Turnout in Senate Elections, 1992–2002

	Model 1		Model 2		Model 3	
	B	S.E.	B	S.E.	B	S.E.
Pres. Election Year	13.45***	1.09	13.07***	1.09	13.44***	1.09
State Turnout Culture	.78***	.08	.79***	.08	.78***	.07
Voting Age Population	−.04	.09	−.05	.08	−.06	.08
Gov. Election Year	1.27	.70	1.12	.69	1.28	.68
Open-Seat Race	−.36	.98	−.24	.97	.08	.96
South	.21	1.00	.01	.99	.10	.98
Percent Over 65	−.28	.18	−.27	.17	−.26	.17
Percent College Educated	−.18*	.09	−.17*	.09	−.14	.09
Percent Rural	−.00	.03	.01	.03	−.00	.03
Percent White	.05	.05	.04	.05	.05	.05
Predicted Closeness	.27**	.10	.25**	.10	.21*	.10
Campaign Intensity	3.53***	.69	.89	1.35	1.09	1.33
Negative Campaigning	−.01	.02	−.08	.04	−.07	.04
Weighted Negative Camp.			.07*	.03	.07*	.03
Percent Independents					.02	.11
Negative Camp. × % Independents					.27	.36
Weighted Negative Camp. × % Independents					−.43*	.19
Constant	40.03***	1.21	40.17***	1.20	39.85***	1.19
Adjusted R²	.83		.83		.84	
Standard Error	4.02		3.97		3.91	

$*p < .05$ $**p < .01$ $***p < .001$

Note: Table entries are OLS coefficients. Weighted negative campaigning is negative campaigning multiplied by spending. All models include dummy variables for election year. $N = 191$.

particular 1992 (with the added stimulus of Perot's first run for the presidency); in states with a history, or "culture," of high turnout; in states where the race was expected to be close; and in states with particularly high-intensity (high-spending) campaigns. Controlling on these other factors, states with a higher proportion of college graduates had lower turnout.

These results generally fit conventional expectations. From our perspective, however, the crucial question is whether the level of negative campaigning in the state will have any noticeable effect on turnout, after controlling on these usual suspects. The demobilization hypothesis predicts a negative coefficient for the campaign tone variable. While the sign of the coefficient in our first model is negative, as reported in past research, the magnitude of the effect is very small and essentially is zero.[1]

Model 1 is a very basic model, however, that implausibly assumes that all voters in all states are equally likely to be exposed to the Senate campaigns. We tried several alternative specifications of the crucial campaign tone variable to relax this implausible assumption. The most logical alternative is that the effects of negative campaigning would be greatest in high-intensity campaigns—that is, in campaigns where the candidates have enough resources to get their message to as many citizens as possible. In other words, the greater the stimulus (i.e., the more likely that voters will be exposed to the campaign), the greater the potential effect.

To examine this possibility, model 2 adds a new interaction term, by multiplying campaign tone by intensity.[2] In essence what we are doing here is weighting the tone of a candidate's campaign by the size of the candidate's campaign budget. As can be seen in model 2 of table 6.1, the picture changes dramatically when we include the interaction term. Campaign negativism turns out to have two different—and offsetting—effects, depending on the nature of the campaign. It has a (not significant) demobilizing effect in low-intensity campaigns and the opposite impact, a significant mobilizing effect, on turnout in high-intensity campaigns, *independent of* the (also positive) effect of campaign intensity itself. These two countervailing effects offset each other so that the predicted total effect of campaign negativism on turnout is again almost nil.

We also tried breaking the campaign tone variable into separate measures of issue-based and person-based negativism. With Kahn and Kenney's (1999a) results in mind, we hypothesized that issue-based criticism of the opponent would typically be viewed as legitimate campaign discourse, and consequently might spur turnout, whereas personal attacks would much more likely be viewed as inappropriate mudslinging and would decrease turnout. Neither of these hypotheses was supported, however. Both issue-based and person-based negativism followed the same patterns as overall levels of negativism, displayed in table 6.1. There were no meaningful differences between the two.

We also tried to capture Kahn and Kenney's "mudslinging effect" by hypothesizing that at relatively moderate levels, increasing campaign negativism may engage, and thus mobilize, many potential voters; but at more extreme levels (where it could be widely perceived as mudslinging), increasing negativism can alienate and hence discourage many potential voters. Such a nonlinear effect can be estimated with a quadratic term (i.e., campaign tone squared), but it too proved to have no additional effect on our basic equation in model 2. We omit these uninteresting results from the table.

One final refinement did bear fruit. Ansolabehere et al. (1994) suggested that negative campaigning was particularly demobilizing for independents. One can imagine that partisans might be energized by negative campaigning, perhaps because of increased anxiety if they believed charges made by their candidates, perhaps by anger at the attacks of the other party's candidates. Independents, without a partisan cause, could simply be turned off by the entire campaign. To test this hypothesis, model 3 introduces three new variables to our model: the percent independents living in each state, the interaction of percent independents with campaign tone, and the interaction of percent independents with campaign tone weighted by spending. This last term proves to be statistically significant, and its sign is consistent with the hypothesis. In states with many independents, much negative campaigning, and much spending, voters are indeed more likely to avoid the polling booths.

Figure 6.1 illustrates these latter effects. In states with relatively large numbers of independents (shown in figure 6.1a), turnout is predicted to be about one point higher in very positive campaigns relative to very negative campaigns. Campaign intensity also plays an important role in encouraging turnout, as relatively high-intensity campaigns have about 3 percent higher turnout than low-intensity campaigns, all else equal. But campaign intensity and campaign tone do not interact with each other, as shown by the three mostly parallel lines in the figure. In states with relatively high levels of partisans, on the other hand (shown in figure 6.1b), an interaction between campaign intensity and campaign tone can be clearly seen. At relatively low levels of campaign intensity, turnout is predicted to be about a point higher in the most positive, relative to the most negative, campaigns. In high-intensity campaigns, however, turnout is predicted to be about two points higher in the most negative campaigns. Thus partisans are stimulated by campaign negativism, while independents are more often turned off.

Effects on Individuals: Survey Data

Turnout is an aggregate or statewide phenomenon, matching perfectly the statewide character of Senate campaigns. But the *decision* of whether to vote is an *individual* one, and any attempts to model that decision at the aggre-

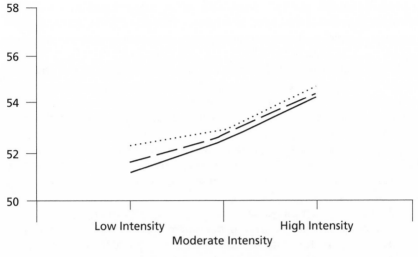

A. High Levels of Independents

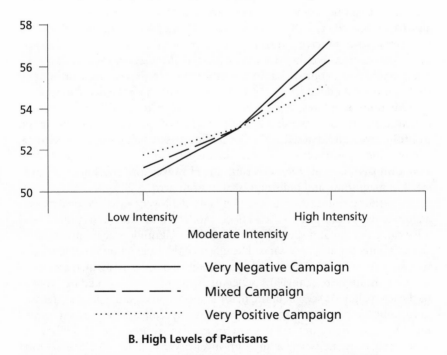

—————————— Very Negative Campaign

— — — — - Mixed Campaign

················· Very Positive Campaign

B. High Levels of Partisans

Figure 6.1   Net Effect of Overall Campaign Negativism on Percent Turnout, Aggregate Level

gate level may risk serious "specification error" (Achen and Shively 1995). For example, we are assuming in figures 6.1a and 6.1b that the individual partisans and independents are causing the effects we observe, but that may not be the case. We can never know for sure with aggregate data. Moreover, aggregate analysis necessarily slights the possibly critical impact of the mass media. The difficulties of detecting media effects, challenging in the best of circumstances, are exacerbated with aggregate-level data (Bartels 1993). For a fuller analysis, we conceptually replicated the aggregate variables reported in table 6.1 with an individual-level data set constructed by combining the ANES data on the 1992 to 2002 Senate elections. This combined data set includes individual-level data from citizens exposed to 150 of the 191 Senate campaigns for which we have campaign tone data, spread fairly evenly across the six election years.

The results of our individual-level analyses are shown in table 6.2. Most of the control variables in the equation are statistically significant and have the expected sign. Turnout is noticeably higher in presidential election years and in states with a history of high turnout. Strength of party identification, the intensity of the campaign in the state, and exposure to the campaign all have strong positive effects on turnout. Likewise age, education, income, race, marital status, home ownership, and length of time in the community all have their predicted effects on turnout. All else equal, a governor's race in the state does not increase turnout, however, nor does an open-seat election in the Senate race. Neither does the expected closeness of the race have any effect on turnout, controlling on the other variables in the equation. But all told, our basic model does an excellent job of explaining the decision to vote.

Our primary interest is the effect of campaign tone. The first model in table 6.2 also includes the simple additive effect of total campaign negativism from the two candidates. Unlike the finding based on aggregate-level data, here we find a *positive* effect of increasing negativism on turnout; a more negative campaign actually increases turnout. However, the effect again is quite small in magnitude and indistinguishable from zero.

As with the aggregate data, this initial model is very basic and provides no adequate test of campaign tone's effect. Model 2 adds the interaction of negative campaigning and spending because this weighting is again necessary to detect significant effects of tone. The effect of the interaction variable is positive, so the model predicts that increased campaign negativism increases turnout in high-intensity campaigns, when many more citizens would be exposed to the campaign. As seen in figure 6.2, the model predicts a 3 percent *decrease* in turnout (i.e., demobilization) with increasing campaign negativism in low-intensity campaigns, but a 4 percent *increase* in turnout (i.e., mobilization) with increasing negativism in high-intensity campaigns.[3] Because low-intensity campaigns are typically noncompetitive to begin with, any decrease in turnout of this magnitude is extremely unlikely to make any difference in

Table 6.2   Individual-Level Turnout in Senate Elections, 1992–2002

	Model 1		Model 2		Model 3	
	B	S.E.	B	S.E.	B	S.E.
Pres. Election Year	.312***	.143	.235	.146	.234	.146
State Turnout Culture	.057***	.009	.052***	.009	.057***	.009
Voting-Age Population	.024***	.007	.023***	.007	.022**	.007
Gov. Election Year	−.090	.086	−.088	.086	−.087	.086
Open-Seat Election	.075	.110	.078	.110	.073	.110
South	.084	.099	.056	.099	.050	.100
Age	.019***	.002	.019***	.002	.019***	.002
Education	.217***	.014	.217***	.014	.218***	.014
Income	.004***	.001	.004***	.001	.004***	.001
Nonwhite	−.220**	.087	−.220**	.087	−.214**	.087
Married	.305***	.068	.304***	.068	.313***	.068
New in Community	−.707***	.127	−.708***	.128	−.705***	.128
Home Owner	.522***	.075	.518***	.075	.514***	.075
Predicted Closeness	−.001	.012	−.004	.012	−.003	.012
Campaign Intensity	.336***	.100	−.148	.200	−.044	.208
Strength of Party ID	1.229***	.101	1.229***	.101	1.233***	.101
Campaign Exposure	1.321***	.071	1.321***	.071	.886**	.307
Negative Campaigning	.001	.003	−.009	.005	−.007	.005
Weighted Negative Camp.			.013**	.005	.010*	.005
Neg. Camp. × Exposure					.015@	.009
Spending × Exposure					.858	.397
Weighted Negative Camp. × Exposure					−.026**	.010
Constant	−.923***	.193	−.908***	.193	−.888***	.196
Model Chi-Square	2082.35***		2090.17***		2098.50***	
Nagelkerke Pseudo R²	.39		.39		.39	
Percent Correctly Classified	76.3%		76.6%		76.5%	

@ $p < .10$ * $p < .05$ ** $p < .01$ *** $p < .001$
Note: Table entries are logistic regression coefficients. Weighted negative campaigning is negative campaigning multiplied by spending. All models include dummy variables for election year. $N = 6,403$.

the outcome of the election. But high-intensity races tend to be much closer, and an increase in the size of the electorate by 4 percent could well make a difference in close races.

So far we have not gone beyond our aggregate data in determining the effect of campaign exposure. We used campaign intensity as a suggestive indicator of exposure. With individual-level data we can do a much better job of discriminating between those more or less exposed to the campaign by considering individual-level measures of likely exposure. As described in appendix B, we constructed such a measure by combining questions about individuals' general interest in the campaign and their attention to national news on television and in newspapers. This scale was already included in our base model, but model 3 adds two important interaction terms: (1) between

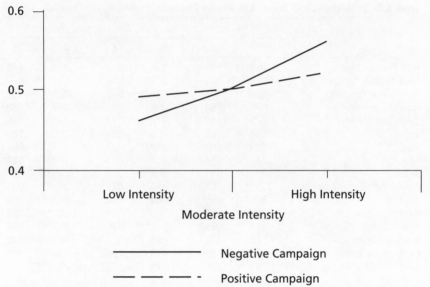

Figure 6.2   Interaction of Campaign Tone and Campaign Spending on Probability of Voting, Individual Level

campaign tone and this direct measure of campaign exposure and (2) interaction among tone, exposure, and spending.[4] Whatever effect the campaign's tone may have on turnout should be magnified by both spending and exposure to the campaign. Indeed, there is no theoretical reason for campaign tone to have *any* effect on potential voters who live in states with low-intensity campaigns and who are barely if at all exposed to the campaign.

As can be seen in the last columns of table 6.2, the interactions with campaign exposure have a large effect on the model, as all of the interaction terms are significant (or nearly so). However, because all of the interactions appear significant, the separate effects of the different variables involved in the interaction can be difficult to understand. Figure 6.3 makes the nature of the interactions easier to appreciate. Figure 6.3a shows how campaign spending and campaign negativism affect turnout among voters who pay almost no attention to politics or national news. For these voters, negative campaigning suppresses turnout by about 4 percent in very low-intensity (i.e., noncompetitive) races but increases turnout by about 8 percent in high-intensity elections. The same pattern holds at average levels of exposure to the campaign, although the magnitude of the differences, as shown in figure 6.3b, is attenuated. Now negative campaigning suppresses turnout by about 2 percent in low-intensity, noncompetitive races, while it increases turnout by 3 percent in high-intensity races. Only at very high levels of exposure to the campaign, shown in figure 6.3c, do we see any reversal of this trend, where negative

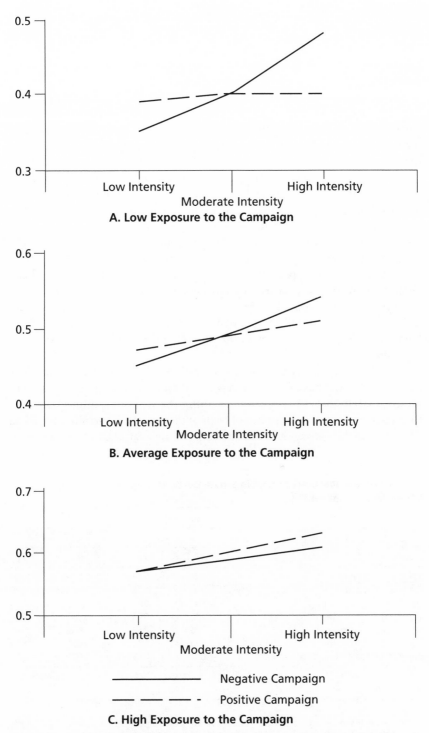

Figure 6.3   Net Effect of Overall Campaign Negativism on Probability of Voting, Individual Level

campaigning is predicted to decrease turnout about 2 percent in the most intense races.[5]

In the aggregate data, we found a strong interaction between the percentage independents living in a state and the effect of campaign negativism, apparently confirming the hypothesis that campaign negativism stimulates turnout among partisans but depresses it among independents. We can test that hypothesis much more convincingly with the individual-level data because we can tie levels of partisanship to individual survey respondents. The easiest way to do this is to split our sample by partisanship, distinguishing independents from partisans, and run model 3 again in each subsample. Table 6.3 reports the crucial results. As can be seen in the table, the pattern of results is similar in the two subsamples but noticeably stronger for the independents. Indeed, none of the interaction terms are significant among partisans. Thus the demobilization and mobilization effects we have been describing are driven primarily by independents. All voters are more likely to turn out when exposed more to media coverage—hardly a surprise. But independents are most likely to abstain in the face of negative campaigning, higher spending, and media exposure. But all of these effects are modest and not consistently in one direction.

Finally, we briefly report some nonfindings. We estimated models that distinguish between issue-based and person-based criticisms of the opponent. Unfortunately, having two variables doing the work of a single campaign tone measure weakens the power of both of them to detect significant effects. The two variables always had the same sign in the analyses, but one was typi-

Table 6.3   Individual-Level Turnout in Senate Elections, 1992–2002, Controlling for Partisanship

| | Independents | | Partisans | |
| | Model 3 | | Model 3 | |
	B	S.E.	B	S.E.
Campaign Intensity	−.144	.337	.027	.269
Campaign Exposure	.788	.516	.973**	.390
Negative Campaigning	−.013	.008	−.003	.006
Weighted Negative Camp.	.017*	.008	.006	.006
Neg. Camp. × Exposure	.022	.015	.009	.011
Spending × Exposure	1.117@	.642	.461	.519
Weighted Negative Camp. × Exposure	−.030@	.016	−.019	.013
N	2,357		4,040	
Nagelkerke R^2	.45		.33	

@$p < .10$ *$p < .05$ **$p < .01$
Note: Table entries are logistic regression coefficients. Weighted negative campaigning is negative campaigning multiplied by spending. Both models include all of the variables from model 3 of table 5.2.

cally significant while the other was not. In model 2, weighted issue-based negative campaigning stimulated turnout, much more so than person-based attacks. But in model 3, where we control for exposure to the campaign, person-based negative campaigning had the stronger effects in the equation. We do not think these results are reliable enough to merit much attention.[6]

We also tried again to replicate Kahn and Kenney's (1999a) mudslinging effect by focusing exclusively on person-based negativism and by looking for curvilinear effects in our overall data. Considering just person-based attacks (and dropping any reference to issues) produces no significant effects for campaign tone. Similarly, including a quadratic term to see if the effects of campaign tone reverse at very high levels of campaign negativism proved to be a bust. We found nothing approaching a significant effect for the quadratic term, whether considering all attacks or focusing exclusively on personal attacks. Whatever Kahn and Kenney are measuring with the mudslinging variable, we cannot locate it with our data.

Effects of Negative Campaigning on System Support

Our examination of negative campaigning has not yet revealed harmful impacts to the American political system. To the extent that political health depends on a large turnout of voters, negative campaigning clearly cannot be held responsible for the low rate of citizen participation in elections, nor for the decrease in turnout in recent decades.

It is possible, however, that we have not yet looked at the right factors. Perhaps there are more subtle deleterious effects to negative campaigning. Perhaps citizens still vote but are less supportive of their government in their attitudes. We will briefly examine this possibility with available and relevant data. Beyond electoral behavior, negative campaigning may have systemic effects that cannot be readily tested. This is speculative, but we will attempt some brief discussion.

We will examine these possibilities after summarizing the effects of negativism on turnout. We found fairly consistent evidence that negative campaigning in Senate elections has at best quite modest effects on turnout, that *mobilizing* effects are at least as likely as *demobilizing* effects, and that independents seem more strongly affected by the tone of the campaign than are partisans. This evidence comes from 191 different election campaigns and more than 6,400 survey respondents across six different election years, and the results are substantively quite similar across two levels of analysis. We will attempt to specify the magnitude of this effect, but it is not a simple task. The answer depends on individual variation in the propensity to vote, irrespective of the nature of the campaign, and on assumptions about variation in campaign negativism.

Figure 6.3 is a good vehicle for putting the limited magnitude of these effects in perspective. Ignoring individual differences in exposure to the campaign and campaign tone, the most likely effect of campaign intensity is to increase turnout by about 6.5 percent.[7] Our estimate is based on two-thirds of the Senate races, where spending varied from a low of 80 cents per capita to a high of $3.78 per capita. If we extend the estimates, albeit too broadly, to include differences between the least and most intense campaigns in our sample, the effect increases to more than 18 percent. This latter estimate could be considered an upper bound on the effect of spending, but it is based on extreme cases.

Ignoring campaign intensity and campaign tone, the effect of individual differences in exposure to the campaign—estimated, remember, by general interest in the campaign and following national news on television and in the newspapers—is 19 percent at the most appropriate estimate and almost 30 percent at the extremes of the observed values of campaign exposure. Individual differences in the propensity to vote (and this is only one individual difference, albeit one of the most important) thus are about three times more important than campaign intensity (i.e., spending) in getting people to the polls.

Ignoring campaign intensity and campaign exposure, the tone of the campaign *by itself* has almost no effect on turnout. We estimate a mobilization "effect" (if one can call it that) of two-tenths of 1 percent, or at the extreme levels of campaign negativism observed in our data, campaign negativism will increase turnout by about 5.5 percent, all else equal.

Two-tenths of 1 percent—the most likely impact of campaign negativity—does not sound like much, particularly when compared with the effects of campaign intensity and individual differences in exposure to the campaign. However, with the average voting age population (VAP) of the states in our sample of just over four million, this works out to an average of 8,176 voters per election who would otherwise not have voted. Six of the Senate elections in our data set were decided by a smaller margin than that, as were six statewide races in the last presidential election. Small effects, then, but potentially consequential effects nonetheless.

The highly nuanced effect of campaign tone on turnout, qualified as it is by campaign intensity, partisanship, and individual differences in exposure to the campaign, may help explain some of the inconsistencies in the literature on the effects of negative campaigning on turnout. Altogether we found relatively few circumstances, and relatively few citizens, who were so turned off by negative campaigning that they stayed home when they otherwise would have voted. At the very least, these data should lay to rest any worries that negative campaigning *in and of itself* demobilizes the electorate—at least in Senate election campaigns.

Political Efficacy and Trust in Government

Let us now go beyond turnout to look at citizen attitudes toward the political system. Our survey data includes questions on voters' sense of political efficacy and their trust in government.[8] If negative campaigning undermines these attitudes, it would also weaken the fundamental allegiance necessary for effective government. As reviewed in chapter 2, a small number of extant studies have examined these relationships. We test this relationship by analyzing the impact of negative campaigning on these attitudes.

First, what is the logic for negative campaigning undermining either of these basic political attitudes? For trust in government, the logic is clear. If one believes all the negative messages, many candidates are crooks, waste taxpayer money, cater to special interests, and rarely can be trusted to do what is right. It seems obvious that the more citizens are exposed to such messages, the less they should trust government generally. The argument for negative campaigning affecting political efficacy takes one more step but is almost as clear. People do not like negative campaigning, the argument goes. If candidates nonetheless engage in it, then it becomes more and more obvious that politicians don't care what people like our survey respondents think, and clear that common people have no say in how government is run. Thus again, the more people are exposed to negative campaigning, the lower should be their general sense of political efficacy.

Table 6.4 reports the crucial campaign variables from analyses where standard measures of political efficacy and trust in government were regressed on the same set of predictors used in model 3 from table 6.2. Negative campaigning should have its strongest effect among respondents who pay a great deal of attention to politics, in high-intensity campaigns. This is the last variable shown in the table; theoretically, we expected negative coefficients. As seen in the first columns of the table, this crucial interaction term does have the hypothesized negative effect on political efficacy, an effect that is larger than its standard error but still not statistically significant.

But we also checked to see if this effect would be stronger among independents by running the analysis separately for partisans and independents. As can be seen in the next columns of the table, this refined hypothesis was supported. Among partisans, negative campaigning has absolutely no effect on levels of political efficacy. But among independents, negative campaigning has the hypothesized negative effect on efficacy for respondents who pay a lot of attention to the campaign and live in states where campaign intensity is high. This effect is statistically significant, one-tailed, but of limited practical significance.

We estimate that political efficacy is about .17 (on a 0–4 scale) lower among independents who pay a great deal of attention to the campaign and

Table 6.4   Effect of Negative Campaigning on Political Efficacy and Trust in Government

	Political Efficacy						Trust in Government	
	All Cases		Independents		Partisans		All Cases	
	B	S.E.	B	S.E.	B	S.E.	B	S.E.
Campaign Intensity	.001	.085	−.131	.140	.125	.109	.038	.072
Campaign Exposure	.048	.125	−.043	.209	.128*	.159	−.055	.105
Negative Campaigning	−.001	.002	−.004	.003	.000	.003	.000	.002
Weighted Negative Camp.	.001	.002	.003	.003	−.002	.003	.001	.002
Neg. Camp. × Exposure	.006@	.003	.008	.006	.004	.004	.002	.003
Spending × Exposure	.211	.154	.399	.247	−.009	.201	.062	.130
Weighted Negative Camp. × Exposure	−.005	.004	−.011@	.006	−.000	.005	−.001	.003
N	6,283		2,333		3,950		6,284	
Adjusted R²	.141		.118		.147		.080	

@ $p < .10$ * $p < .05$
Note: Table entries are 2SLS coefficients. Weighted negative campaigning is negative campaigning multiplied by spending. All models include all of the variables from model 3 of table 5.2, plus the standard measure of liberalism-conservatism and a scale tapping preference for more or less government spending.

live in a state with a high-intensity, fairly negative Senate campaign, compared with independents who pay little attention to politics and who live in states with relatively positive, low-intensity Senate races. Of course, we are considering the effect of only one election campaign on a fairly general political attitude. Gubernatorial campaigns should have just as much effect as Senate campaigns, and presidential campaigns should have a greater effect than either of them. Making a number of fairly stringent assumptions (that the effects we estimated here accumulate in an additive manner across many different campaigns), it is not hard to imagine that negative campaigning could have a large cumulative effect on political efficacy.

The results for trust in government are shown in the last columns of table 6.4. There is no hint whatsoever in the data that the tone of political campaigns has any effect on levels of trust in government. The data look no different if we consider just independents or just partisans. The logic that negative campaigns might lower trust in government is clear, but the evidence, at least in our data, simply does not exist.

There are still more general, and less quantifiable, potential effects of campaign negativity. It may be that the tone of government comes to reflect the harshness of elections. Many members of the Senate, and the House, have commented on the loss of civility in legislative proceedings in recent years. This change probably results from many causes—including cultural trends, close partisan competition for national office, and the personal style of individual leaders. It may also be true that candidates who survive or conduct negative campaigns are prone to carry that battle mode into the halls of Congress.

Another effect may be recruitment of candidates. Both political parties have reported difficulty recruiting candidates for Senate races, despite the many perquisites of the office (Dewar 2003). Knowing of the travails of contemporary campaigning (as well as the expense), it may well be that prospective aspirants decline to endure the negative examinations of their records, personal lives, and political correctness that have become characteristic of campaigns. We would worry if the electoral process was in effect closing the doors of office to any significant number of decent, capable, and dedicated individuals. We have no *evidence* that those effects are widespread, but we still may have reason to worry about the future health of the republic.

Notes

This chapter draws on material originally published as Richard R. Lau and Gerald M. Pomper, "Effects of Negative Campaigning on Turnout in U.S. Senate Elections, 1988–1998," *Journal of Politics* 63 (August 2001): 804–819.

1. Because our measures of the nature of the campaign were based on a coding of statements from campaign officials reported in the newspapers, and because the number of articles about the campaigns (and thus the number of statements on which our means were based) differed across campaigns, we were concerned that the reliability of the measure of campaign tone could vary across campaigns, which could lead to heteroskedasticity. We therefore conducted White's (1980) test of heteroskedasticity for each equation considered, using as predictors (along with all the independent variables included in the models) the number of statements coded from each campaign. In no case did heteroskedasticity appear to be a problem, and we therefore report the familiar OLS results. The substantive findings do not change if the models in table 6.1 are estimated with weighted least squares (WLS).

2. Because spending across candidates is by no means equal, this new variable was actually created by multiplying the negativism of the Democrat's campaign by the log of his or her spending per capita, and adding that to the product of the negativism of the Republican's campaign multiplied by the log of his or her spending per capita. Thus if one of the candidates had disproportionate resources to get his or her message across, the negativism of that message counted disproportionately in the overall measure of weighted campaign tone for the state.

3. These (and subsequent) probabilities from the logistic regressions are predicted for "average" respondents. Our hypothetical average respondent is forty years old, has a high school education, and lives in a household earning about $38,000 a year. She is a white, married home owner who has lived in her community for at least two years, with moderate campaign exposure. The race is pre-

dicted to be moderately close, and the candidates spend the median amount per capita in the state. There is a gubernatorial race in this nonsouthern state.

4. For statistical reasons we must also add the interaction between campaign intensity (spending) and campaign exposure.

5. The reader should notice that the scale on the vertical axis changes as we move from figure 6.3a to 6.3b and then to 6.3c, which tends to obscure the effect of campaign exposure on turnout. On average, turnout is about 10 percent higher for those with high levels of campaign exposure compared with those with average levels of campaign exposure, who in turn are about 10 percent more likely to vote than respondents with low levels of campaign exposure.

6. These results are available on our website (http://fas-polisci.rutgers.edu/ ~lau/) for interested readers.

7. We measure intensity as the logarithm of campaign spending per capita. The difference reported here is based on estimates at the 17th and 83rd percentile of spending in all the Senate races in our data. These boundaries are also used in the discussion of the effects of campaign exposure and campaign tone on turnout.

8. Political efficacy is measured by the extent of disagreement with two statements: "People like me don't have any say about what the government does," and "I don't think public officials care much what people like me think." We averaged the responses to these two statements. Trust in government was measured by responses to four questions: "Do you think that people in the government waste a lot of money we pay in taxes, waste some of it, or don't waste very much of it?" "How much of the time do you think you can trust the government in Washington to do what is right?" "Would you say the government is pretty much run by a few big interests looking out for themselves or that it is run for the benefit of all the people?" and "Do you think that quite a few of the people running the government are crooked, not very many are, or do you think hardly any of them are crooked?"

Normative Thoughts on Negative Campaigning 7

T HE PRECEDING CHAPTERS probed the empirical realities of negative campaigning. We tested, and disputed, much of the conventional
wisdom. In this concluding chapter, we first summarize our major
findings. Then, speculating beyond the empirical realities, we advance some
thoughts on possible improvements in the campaign process.

Our research leads to the following empirical conclusions:

- The previous literature on negative campaigning provides no clear evi-
dentiary base for either the unusual effectiveness of the technique or its
presumed deleterious effects on the political system. There are relatively
few high-quality studies of actual elections with representative samples
of voters.
- Negative campaigning is less prevalent than commonly believed. It var-
ies by campaign situation, party, and gender.
- Negative campaigning is generally not very effective in drawing votes,
and then only in some situations. The practice hurts incumbents; at best
it aids challengers only slightly.
- There is no consistent pattern to the effects of negative campaigns for
open seats. Generally speaking, going negative helps candidates a little
when they have relatively few campaign resources compared with their
opponents, but the strategy hurts candidates when they have more
money than their opponents.
- We found very limited evidence that attacking an opponent on the
issues was a more effective strategy than attacking an opponent on a
more personal nature. In general, however, we could detect no difference in the impact of the two attack modes.
- Negative campaigning does not generally reduce turnout; when combined with high levels of spending, it may actually increase turnout.
However, independents as a group are much more likely than Democrats or Republicans to be turned off by negative campaigning and consequently to stay at home on election day.
- Negative campaigning has no detectable effect on trust in government.
It may lower political efficacy, but, again, only among political independents.

Further Speculations

We now go beyond our data analysis to twice ask, "*Should* we have negative campaigns?" We then recommend some means to limit the baleful effects of these campaigns, even as we recognize, and seek to increase, their contributions to political debate.

In practical terms, our results suggest that campaigners might be *unwise* to engage in such tactics. Choosing to attack an opponent, our data suggest, probably provokes a counterattack, undermining any effectiveness of such a campaign strategy. Our campaign data do not have the dynamic element that would allow us to comment on strategic advantages in the *timing* of negative attacks on an opponent (and the timing of responses), but we can say that a one-for-one response, *some time* during the campaign, seems almost inevitable. As Richard Fenno reports, "'The wrong lesson,' advised media consultant Frank Greer, 'is that negative campaigns work. The right lesson is that if you stand up and fight back, you can beat them. If you don't, you'll lose'" (Fenno 1996, 208).

An even more persuasive instrumentalist argument may be available. Negative campaigning *should* be less attractive to candidates (and their campaign managers) if, contrary to conventional wisdom, the practice is not a particularly effective campaign technique. As the previous analyses have shown, negativism is no guarantee of success, and it is often associated with loss of votes, not gain.

We ask again, however, but now normatively, if we *should* discourage negative campaigning. Before we pursue that effort too far, we might acknowledge some merits in the practice. Negative campaigning is not lying and stealing and cheating; it is criticizing the opponent. From a normative point of view, it is not at all clear that we *should* try to reduce negative campaigning—at least issue-based negative campaigning.

The standard for evaluating negative campaigning is the public's interest, not the candidates' interests. It is therefore irrelevant whether negative campaigning works, or that it often is ineffective, as seen in the analyses of chapters 4 and 5. The purpose of democracy is popular control; its desired means is what Woodrow Wilson termed "government by discussion" and what John Dewey meant when he wrote, "Democracy is about talk." In an effective democracy, we must judge—and, if possible, structure—campaigns so that they serve an "informing function" and "help voters make rational voting decisions." These decisions will be more rational, Kelley elaborates, when voters have "full information about the alternatives to be voted upon [and] full knowledge of all the effects that would attend the choice of each alternative" (Kelley 1960, 8–10).

Campaign appeals—including negative appeals—will promote rational voting, Kelley suggests, to the extent that they are accurate, expose voters to reasons for supporting each candidate, clarify differences among these candidates, and identify sources. Candidates, who are essentially self-interested, may not want to foster rational voting, but that is no reason to neglect the public's interest in rationality. "That the participants in public discussion put effectiveness before truth is not something that in and of itself means that they cannot be made to serve truth" (Kelley 1960, 21–23).

We should emphasize that such rational campaign discussion is not equivalent to an exclusive focus on policy issues. A voter can properly concentrate on personal features of candidates, not just their programs, because personal characteristics do affect government. Voters will want officials who are honest rather than corrupt, capable rather than inept, compassionate rather than indifferent (Salmore and Salmore 1989, 113). Campaigns may properly include negative comments about these characteristics.

Despite the widespread disapproval of negative campaigning, there may be, ironically, positive features to it. West (1993, 51) found in his study of advertisements from 1952 to 1992 that "the most substantive appeals actually came in negative spots," and "in recent years domestic performance and specific policy statements more than personal qualities have been the object of the negative prominent ads." Likewise, Geer (2000) shows that issues are more commonly stressed in negative rather than positive advertisements, and further that the claims made in attack ads are more often backed by verifiable evidence than the claims made in positive ads (Geer 2003). This would suggest that negative ads—and negative campaigning more generally, if it followed that same pattern—are *good* for democracy.

Elections are about choices, not courtesy. The point of an election campaign is to educate voters about the differences between the candidates, at least the differences that are relevant to the performance of the job. It is difficult to imagine how this goal can be accomplished unless candidates contrast their own proposals and accomplishments with those of their opponents. Even some "personal attacks" could be considered a legitimate part of the decision-making process (e.g., "My opponent does not have the experience for this job"). If we want to improve campaign discourse we might try to discourage person- or character-based attacks of the opponent that have little to do with a candidate's ability to perform the job, but we see no reason to discourage issue-based attacks, nor all types of person-based attacks.

We can also frankly recognize that in many instances we *should* want candidates to engage in negative campaigning. When an incumbent has a poor record in a particular area, shouldn't she be held accountable for it? If a candidate makes a wrongheaded proposal, shouldn't he be taken to task for it? In such instances, criticism of an opponent is a healthy, legitimate part of democratic dialogue. Campaign lies and distortions are unhealthy for democracy and should be discouraged as much as possible, but this adage is equally true whether the lies are aimed at an opponent or used to falsify a candidate's own merits. Better campaigning requires better discourse, however phrased (Simon 2002). Our goal should be better politics, not more refined politesse.

Indeed, one could make the case that negative campaigning is actually good for democracy. William Mayer presents a trenchant position along these lines, arguing that "any serious, substantive discussion of what a candidate intends to do after the election can only be conducted by talking about the flaws and shortcomings of current policies." Furthermore, he points out that voters need to know not only about candidates' claimed merits but also about "the abilities and virtues they don't have; the mistakes they have made; the problems they haven't dealt with; the issues they would prefer not to talk about; the bad or unrealistic policies they have proposed" (Mayer 1996, 441).

Two Faces of Negative Campaigning

We now go beyond our data to speculate on possible improvements in election campaigns. We know that our recommendations will not make politics perfect, and we cannot prove with the data available to us that they will even make it better. Still, we hope we can contribute to a useful discussion.

We begin this discussion by illustrating the duality of negative campaigning, its combination of potential contributions and defects. Our focus is a single Senate race, the 1996 contest in Massachusetts between incumbent Democrat John F. Kerry, seeking his third term, and his Republican challenger, sitting governor William F. Weld.

The race featured two distinguished politicians, each with extensive experience in government, "intelligent, articulate, artful and passionate about their conflicting visions, . . . two Daniel Websters treading the boards." In a commitment to public understanding, they agreed to limit their spending to $5 million and to engage in seven televised debates; observers called their competition "the most intelligent Senate race in the country" (Nyhan 1996).

But the contest was not all philosophic dialogue. It ultimately involved considerable and mutual attacks from Kerry and Weld, illustrating both the good, smiling face of negative campaigning and its harsh, snarling aspect.

The last of the debates, at historic Faneuil Hall in Boston, showed the attractive face, even as the candidates made sharp attacks. Local reporters (Aucoin and Phillips 1996) described the debate:

> In a crackling finale to their epic series of debates, U.S. Sen. John F. Kerry and Gov. William F. Weld last night gave Massachusetts voters a memorable reminder of the stark choice they will confront in the voting booth one week from today.
>
> Kerry and Weld restated the themes that have animated their yearlong campaign—a commitment to tax equity and economic

fairness by the senator, a commitment to tax cuts and scaled-back government by the governor—but did so with a fervor and sharpness designed to reach the crucial bloc of undecided voters in what polls show is a deadlocked race. . . .

Kerry accused Weld of opposing policies that help working people, the elderly and college students and of proposing tax cuts that primarily benefit the wealthy. Weld fired back with selections from Kerry's voting record that he said prove the senator opposes tough crime laws, welfare reform and a balanced budget while supporting tax increases.

Partisan intensity permeated the event, both inside the hall—where the candidates were repeatedly interrupted by raucous applause—and out, where thousands of supporters of each candidate shouted and waved signs. . . .

But the candidates needed no help in keeping the emotional temperature high. It rose to an especially searing level when Kerry alluded to the deaths of two young children in foster care and accused Weld of using funds designated for hiring social workers to pay for an election-year tax cut. . . .

Weld continued to jab at Kerry over a *Globe* report on the senator's free use, on and off for several months in the 1980s, of the posh Washington apartment of a top lobbying firm official, his acceptance of reduced-rate housing from two developers, and his failure to pay for a leased car for 16 months. "This issue of the freebies is relevant," Weld said, because Kerry would be "more attuned" to the stress on taxpayers if he had not received such perks. . . .

Between attacks on each other, the pair touted their achievements.

Kerry pointed to his sponsorship of an anticrime bill designed to put 100,000 new police officers on the streets, and noted that 1,658 have already been hired in Massachusetts. He said the deficit-reduction plan he supported has helped create 10.5 million new jobs, spoke of his fight to save $2.7 billion in education funds GOP leaders had targeted for elimination, and noted that he had supported an increase in the minimum wage.

Weld, for his part, noted that unemployment has dropped from 10 percent to 4 percent since he became governor in 1990, with 250,000 new jobs created; that there has been a 28 percent drop in the welfare rolls since he signed a new welfare reform law; and that the state is now spending $1.2 billion more per year on K–12 education.

The debate included negative comments, but it generally contributed to an informed decision by the voters. The candidates demonstrated their policy differences, referring to specific issues, and their criticisms of the opposing candidate were directly related to those public questions. When they dealt with personal characteristics, the characteristics were relevant to official duties—such as Weld's alleged lack of compassion or Kerry's alleged ethical lapses. These negative charges were balanced by each candidate's presentation of his own positive appeals. Notably, the debate engaged public attention, both emotionally and intellectually.

The less appealing face of negative campaigning showed itself in television ads sponsored by the candidates. A reporter (Grunwald 1996) deplored this part of the campaign:

> On television, the choice for U.S. Senate is clear.
>
> You can vote for the heartless liar who wants to destroy the environment, shred Medicare, attack innocent children and throw Grandma on the street.
>
> Or you can vote for the tax-happy freeloader who supports cop killers, terrorists, drug addicts, welfare cheats, gang members, unemployment and gridlock. . . .
>
> One way to gauge their effect is to look at how the image of these two men, as measured in opinion polls, has shifted through the year. Both are now substantially less popular than they were 11 months ago, when Weld announced his Senate campaign.
>
> Fewer voters now admire Weld's work as governor. Fewer think Kerry has earned another term in office. Two widely admired public figures have taken each another down a notch. . . .
>
> This air war did not begin as a dogfight. In fact, the candidates launched their ad blitzes this summer with entirely positive messages.
>
> Weld kicked off with a testimonial from a single mom hailing his crusade against deadbeat dads. He followed up with a biographical spot highlighting his independence from Republicans (quitting the Reagan administration, standing up for abortion rights at the 1992 convention) and cooperation with Democrats (enacting welfare reform, balancing the budget). Both ads featured upbeat music, bright colors, and the governor kissing babies.
>
> Kerry then went up with a bio of his own. It began with footage of a shaggy-haired Kerry serving in Vietnam, testifying against the war, and skating around in ill-fitting hockey gear.
>
> Then it detailed some of his accomplishments: fighting for 100,000 new cops, the minimum wage, tax breaks for small businesses. Finally, a slogan: On Duty in the U.S. Senate.

It was all so civil and genteel, with substance for good measure. It didn't last a month. . . .

Pretty soon, Weld was airing dark images of civic dysfunction, pandering to suburban fears of urban decay. A jail door slams. Gang members strut along the train tracks. A junkie drops a needle. An alcoholic drowns his sorrows. . . .

Meanwhile, Kerry was taking shrill to new levels, blasting Republicans for savaging schools, denying children health care, sucking up to tobacco firms and slashing Medicare. He ripped Weld for busting unions and accused him of limiting seniors in nursing homes to a dollar a day. . . .

If you needed a slogan for the air war, you could do a lot worse than the latest slogan for Weld's campaign: "Massachusetts Deserves Better."

Or you could steal a slogan from Kerry's environmental attack ad. It's emblazoned on a barrel in the corner of your TV: "Danger—Toxic Material."

We lack any direct evidence on these campaign events. Perhaps the difference between them reflects only the difference between face-to-face debate and televised advertisements. But the negative material of these ads seems to fall short by a considerable margin of the standards of desirable campaigning. Positive presentations of the candidates' own qualifications and experience were discarded. The bulk of the messages distorted the opponent's record, without offering alternative policy proposals. In reaction, to judge by press reports and opinion polls, dislike of both candidates increased.

Making Use of Negative Campaigning

Seeing such developments in this race between two able and principled candidates makes us infer that the campaign process itself may be faulty, pushing candidates to do their worst, not their best. American campaigns, in their hurly-burly combination of gimmicks, slogans, and rhetoric, do help inform voters. Yet they also have problems that stem from the ways contemporary contests structure the ambitions of competing politicians. By developing some changes in campaigns, we may be able to make use of negative campaigning to improve the electoral process.

We suggest a metaphor. The human circulation system naturally includes cholesterol in two varieties: "bad" (low-density lipoproteins) and "good" (high-density lipoproteins). Individuals may improve their health through such measures as low-fat diets, but society can encourage such behavior through medication, publicity, and regulation (e.g., by requiring that food labels list fat content). In a democracy, the body politic also has a circulatory system—campaigning—that distributes policy and personal appeals to the electorate. Social practices may encourage the good rather than the bad forms of campaigning.

Four features of contemporary electoral competition underlie harmful practices. First, the stakes of electoral competition are very high, especially in races for the U.S. Senate. Victory brings a contestant to the most powerful elective office in the United States other than the presidency; defeat typically means a return to private life without political influence. Second, the resources committed to the competition are immense—emotional investment, financial investment in the tens of millions of dollars, and ideological investment in programs these candidates support. Third, there appear to be great incentives fostering negative campaigning, even its unattractive face, but few for restrained campaigning. Conventional wisdom holds that the first works, but the second is self-defeating. Fourth, there are no evident institutional restraints on harmful tactics; no agency other than the electorate can restrict or punish bad practices.

Any improvement in campaigning will need to recognize these structuring factors. If there is to be any reform, we cannot expect it to come from calls to individual candidates to "be good." Politically ambitious men and women will do what they think necessary or effective in winning office. We must instead follow the lessons of the Constitution and *The Federalist*: "ambition must be made to counteract ambition." To paraphrase James Madison: Because candidates are not angels, the self-interest of the candidates must be connected with informing the public's electoral judgment (Madison 1941 [1787], 337).

Let us speculate on changes in the structure of politics that might induce candidates to use negative campaigning in appropriate rather than unsavory ways. This general principle suggests some specific reforms. If less is at stake in an election, then ambitious candidates will have less reason to offend. A particular step in this direction would be to lessen the financial costs of a campaign to individual candidates, which would also decrease their emotional investment. Public financing of campaigns would bring about these effects, assuring candidates of necessary money and probably reducing total spending. Public financing can even be structured to offset the advantages of individually wealthy candidates who finance their own campaigns.[1] Legislation could also provide all serious contenders with more free resources, such as public service time on television or voter pamphlets distributed at government expense, as in California, Oregon, and other states.

A similar improvement would be a greater role for the political parties in financing campaigns. When campaign money comes from party coffers, individual candidates are relieved of some of the burden of soliciting funds, making promises to contributors, and risking disappointment of their supporters and themselves. However, recent campaign "reform" actually reduces the parties' role by curbing "soft money" and thereby increases the pressures on individual campaigners.

The environment would also change if candidates began their efforts with different assumptions about successful strategies. At present, believing that every form of negative campaigning works, candidates are tempted to use these tactics without discrimination, reinforcing cycles of attack and counterattack. The diffusion of research, such as that in this book, disputing the conventional wisdom that all negative campaigning is effective should alter these strategies. Recall our metaphor: When individuals learn that fatty foods decrease their life expectancy, they may well alter their diets. If candidates learn that inappropriate negativism decreases their political viability, they will probably alter their electoral behavior.

Most important is restructuring campaigns to provide incentives for more appropriate campaigning, in both its negative and positive forms. Some elements that structure campaigns are not subject to ready change—from the First Amendment to the two-party system. But campaign modes are not fixed; they are strategic reactions to a particular environment. They need not be "filled with evasions, distortions, ambiguities, irrelevancies, and calculated efforts to mislead." By recognizing that "the relationship of campaigners to each other and to the campaign audience shapes the strategy of campaigners and hence the content of campaign communications" (Kelley 1960, 146, 154), we make change possible.

For example, if candidates must identify themselves with their advertisements, unfair charges will probably decline. When candidates are mandated to "say it yourself," they are less likely to be reckless and more likely to observe norms of decent dialogue (Pomper and Reed 1999). This principle has been included in recent amendments to the federal campaign finance law, and it has been incorporated in a voluntary fair campaign code developed in New Jersey. It should be extended.

The greatest abuses in campaigns come from anonymous sources and unidentified "front" organizations. Campaigns would be improved if candidates were held responsible for approving all advertisements made on their behalf, even if paid by others, but this approach faces considerable constitutional and practical limitations. A simpler step is available. Without limiting the vigor of campaigns, these organizations can properly be required to identify themselves and their contributors. Monies spent to attack candidates, even in spurious "issue ads," should be considered campaign expenditures and come only from designated electoral funds, not from the general treasuries of corporations, unions, and other groups. The new federal law—recently upheld by the U.S. Supreme Court (*McConnell v. FEC*, 2003)—now properly includes these requirements (Potter and Jowers 2002; Campaign Finance Institute 2003).

Candidate debates combine many of these desirable features. As illustrated by the Kerry–Weld contest, debates can include useful negative campaigning in the form of adverse comments on an opponent's record and qualifications, but debates also inherently limit undesirable behavior. Being on stage together, candidates must take personal responsibility for their negative comments, anonymity is impossible, excesses are inhibited by the norms of face-to-face dialogue, and critical comments can be immediately refuted. Content analysis has shown that debates emphasize policy discussion rather than tactical or personal material, an aid to electoral judgment (Downing 1996).

Structurally, debates also offer the great advantage of giving each candidate exactly the same amount of time, providing the electorate with equal access to information—negative and positive—on each candidate. More debates can be encouraged by requiring candidates to participate as a condition for public funding of their campaigns. Such debates and funding might also encourage more relatively qualified opposition candidates to enter even "hopeless" races in one-party states, promoting greater public awareness and, quite possibly, greater electoral competition.

Incentives toward more appropriate campaigning can also be created by private agencies taking action when it counts during the campaigns. The mass media, for example, have developed "ad watches," by which they examine the claims made in candidates' advertising. In practice, ad watches have proven problematic, sometimes resulting in even further diffusion of unsavory material. Nevertheless, efforts to get independent verification of candidate claims remain attractive. At the very least, the media can judge the factual accuracy of negative campaigning. As Jamieson cogently writes, "Postmodernism aside, at some level, political discourse presupposes the existence of brute, verifiable facts. . . . There either are or are not homeless on the streets. The rate of unemployment has either increased since 1988 or it has not" (Jamieson 1992, 217). Fact-checking is a basic practice of professional journalists that can easily be applied to candidate assessment.

Beyond this minimal test, the media can promote, even if they cannot enforce, other standards of good political discourse: "that argument should be backed by proof, that the fairness and accuracy of the evidence should be subject to scrutiny, that the context from which evidence emerged should not be distorted, that those who are attacked have a right to reply" (Jamieson 1992, 218). The problem is not the existence of negative campaigning, which actually does tend to provide evidence more often than do positive messages (Geer 2003). The proper concern is unfair and inaccurate claims and criticisms, whether phrased in positive or negative terms. Press review can encourage practices that better meet the standards presented by Kelley and Jamieson. Knowing that they may be called to account by these independent observers, campaigners may show a selfish interest in avoiding false, unsubstantiated, and distorted statements.

Another means to improve electioneering is through codes of fair campaign practices. Such codes have been established through legislative or administrative action in Minnesota, Hawaii, and Texas. In the latter state, illustratively, candidates may voluntarily limit negative campaigning by signing the following pledge (Texas Ethics Commission 2003):

> I will conduct the campaign openly and publicly and limit attacks on my opponent to legitimate challenges to my opponent's record and stated positions on issues.
>
> I will not use or permit the use of character defamation, whispering campaigns, libel, slander or scurrilous attacks on any candidate or the candidate's personal or family life.
>
> I will not use or permit any appeal to negative prejudice based on race, sex, religion or national origin.
>
> I will not use campaign material of any sort that misrepresents, distorts, or otherwise falsifies the facts, nor will I use malicious or unfounded accusations that aim at creating or exploiting doubts, without justification, as to the personal integrity or patriotism of my opponent.

State action to enforce these rules carries many difficulties. The general terms of any code will require lengthy interpretation and application, probably running beyond election day. Campaigns may be inhibited from vigorous debate, and free speech rights damaged. Charging code violations may itself become an election tactic, as campaigners accuse their opponents of unfair attacks, creating a new form of negative campaigning.

An alternative method is the creation of citizen organizations to promote better campaigning. In Los Angeles and other cities, for example, the League of Women Voters has established a Campaign Watch Commission to enforce three standards:

> That all candidates and campaigns be free of prejudice based on race, gender, religion, national origin, age or sexual orientation;
>
> That all candidates and campaigns be free of personal character attacks;
>
> That all candidates and campaigns be free of false or misleading statements or accusations.

The League also provides a timely mechanism for enforcement of these standards. Candidates can file brief complaints within ten days of an alleged violation, and opponents are expected to answer within twenty-four hours. The commission decides quickly in one of three ways: taking no action, issuing a warning to the offending candidate, or releasing its findings of a violation to the media (League of Women Voters of Los Angeles 2003).

The League's practice is no panacea for the ills of campaigning, and its procedures can be manipulated by candidates. It offers the great advantage, however, of making campaign practices themselves subject to campaign discussion. By enlisting the self-interest of politicians in the cause of relevant and focused campaign conduct, the League provides a deterrent to bad practices without the heavy hand and delayed action of government. Like ad watches, the effect of such monitoring may be "prophylactic," inducing candidates to be more careful in their behavior to avoid outside censure, self-regulating their campaign diets as it were. As reporters claimed, "Our coverage is keeping the bastards honest. . . . [Perhaps] those who planned commercials really sat around worrying about whether we'd criticize them or not" (Jamieson and Waldman 2000, 108).

Conclusion: Voters and Campaigns

The ultimate check to bad campaigning must come at the ballot box. As Madison taught, "a dependence on the people is the primary control on the government"—and on aspirant governors—although experience has taught us the need for "auxiliary precautions" such as those we propose (Madison 1941 [1787], 337). Voters hold the most effective sanction—punishing candidates who engage in the virulent forms of campaigning. If voters did this consistently, candidates might not become paragons of electoral virtue, but they would change their behavior to better realize their own ambitions.

We must remember that the purpose of campaigning in a democracy is not the election of politicians for their own sake but their election as representatives of the voters. "From a representational standpoint," as argued by Fenno, "the curse of negative campaigning is that it distorts the constituency connection of the winning politician by leaving him or her without strongly positive constituency ties. The winning candidate will have earned the legal right to represent a constituency, but the constituents are left without a clue as to how the incumbent would go about doing it" (Fenno 1996, 265). This strikes us as an interesting, and testable, hypothesis. Some negative campaigns promote accountability, some decrease it, depending on the content of the criticisms. Improving campaigns means improving these linkages, and that goal requires that the electorate be trusted to hear and evaluate both negative and positive campaign appeals.

Concerns about negative campaigning to some extent reflect a dim appraisal of the electorate. Voters must be protected from candidates, this line of argument goes, because they know little about politics and seem to care even less, or they are easily discouraged, or, unable to distinguish truth from lies, they are likely to be fooled by misrepresentations of the past and exaggerations about future consequences. Our data provide no support for such sweeping statements. Contemporary research shows instead that despite their shortcomings, most voters do seem able to vote "correctly" (Lau and Redlawsk 1997).

The benefits and costs of negative campaigning are much more subtle and more nuanced, and the electorate seems reasonably able to detect and respond to at least some of those nuances. There are neither fixed rules for campaigners nor immutable preferences held by voters. Our evidence on the impact of negative campaigning is a testament to the abilities of a mass electorate. It provides one more reason to believe that "the electorate behaves about as rationally and responsibly as we should expect, given the clarity of the alternatives presented to it and the character of the information available to it" (Key and Cummings 1966, 7).

Surely, campaigning can be bettered, and we have offered suggestions for improvement. Scholars like us would probably express a preference for campaigns conducted by exemplary candidates through civil debates, in which statements are always disinterested and truth is always unvarnished. That is to say, we would probably express a preference for campaigns as the model academic seminar. Yet we know that even academia does not now, and probably never did, resemble dispassionate symposia, and it is vain to think that the exuberant world of democratic politics will fit that model any better.

Let us try to make campaigns more fair, statements more accurate, discourse more relevant, politicians more respected, and citizens more interested. And let us encourage researchers to continue studying campaigns—and campaign reform—in a multitude of different settings and with a variety of different methods. But let us not discourage relevant criticism of an opponent because of any unwarranted fears that such attacks are inordinately persuasive or that they inevitably discourage citizen engagement with the political system.

In this volume we examined one aspect of the democratic process, campaigning, particularly negative campaigning. We recall one of the most famous stories about politics, Plato's "Myth of the Cave" (Plato 1945, 228–230). There, men are chained facing a wall, seeing only shadows cast by a fire behind their backs. Unaware of their condition, they cannot recognize reality. "Prisoners so confined would have seen nothing of themselves or one another except the shadows thrown by the fire-light on the wall of the Cave facing them."

The dialogue of democracy at times can seem no more than a dance of such shadows. Candidates often stoke the fires that cast deceptive images before the voters. Truth is hard to achieve, hard to determine, and sometimes hard to accept. But proper campaigning, negative as well as positive, can free citizens from error. Our research leads us to an optimistic conclusion: With all its faults, the republic still stands.

Notes

1. Maine and Vermont provide higher levels of public funding for candidates opposed by self-financing candidates who do not accept this funding. The new federal campaign finance law allows higher contributions to candidates facing rich self-financed opponents.

Appendix A
Description of Studies Included in the Meta-Analysis

Study	Independent Variable	Subjects and Design	Dependent Variables	Results
1. Ansolabehere and Iyengar 1995	Positive or negative ad for actual candidates, inserted into regular commercial break of local news program	Experiment with a convenience sample of 2,216 residents	Intended turnout;	Negative ads depressed intended turnout, $d = -.10$;
			Vote intention in primary election;	Negative ads decreased intended vote for their sponsor during primary elections, $d = -.14$;
			Vote intention in general election;	Negative ads increased vote intention for their sponsor during general elections, $d = .10$;
			Political efficacy	Negative ads decreased efficacy, $d = -.12$.
2. Ansolabehere, Iyengar, Simon, and Valentino 1994	Positive/negative "tone" of 1992 Senate campaigns, coded from newspaper accounts	Aggregate analysis of turnout in 34 Senate elections	Actual turnout	States with more negative Senate election campaigns had lower turnout, $d = -1.39$.
3. Babbitt and Lau 1994	Positive/negative "tone" of 1988 and 1990 Senate campaigns, coded from newspaper accounts	Information about candidates from 1988 and 1990 U.S. Senate elections	Knowledge of major-party candidates running in election	Negative issue-based campaigning associated with more issue-based knowledge of candidates but not more general knowledge about incumbent, average $d = .04$.

(continues)

Study	Independent Variable	Subjects and Design	Dependent Variables	Results
4. Basil, Schooler, and Reeves 1991	Positive and negative ads from two senatorial campaigns in another state	Repeated measures design; convenience sample of 24 local community residents saw two "campaigns" consisting of three positive or three negative ads from each candidate in the Senate election	Affect for sponsor of ad;	Candidate was liked better and perceived as stronger when presented positive ads, $d = -.30$;
			Affect for target of ad;	Target was liked better when the opponent used positive rather than negative ads, $d = .46$;
			Memory for ads	Positive ads were recalled better than negative ads, $d = .30$.
5. Brians and Wattenberg 1996	Exposure to television news, positive ads, and negative ads during the 1992 presidential election	51% of nationally representative survey (ANES data, $N = 1,263$) who could recall some political ad	Memory for ads	Negative political ads more likely to be recalled relative to an estimate of their prevalence during campaign, $d = .51$.
6. Bullock 1994	Exposure to ads for two hypothetical state senate candidates, varying by the type of attack ad (image or issue) and the ambiguity of the ad	Experiment with 451 randomly selected prospective jurors awaiting assignment	Affect for target;	Targeted candidates were rated less favorably after exposure to negative ads compared with positive ads, $d = 1.40$;
			Affect for sponsor;	Candidates were rated more positively when sponsoring positive ads than attack ads, $d = -1.52$;

Study		Measure	Result
7. Capella and Taylor 1992	Which candidate initiated negative ads in 25 1986 Senate campaigns with "substantial amounts of negative advertising"	Vote intention / Vote totals in 25 Senate elections	Negative ads caused the likelihood of voting for the targeted candidate to drop significantly, **d = 1.09**.
		Authors' judgment of whether negative ad campaign "worked" or "failed" (i.e., how final results differed from projected results before ad campaign began)	Negative ad campaign decreased proportion of vote obtained by initiator of negative ads in 18 of 25 elections, **d = −.58**.
8. Finkel and Geer 1998	Proportion of negative ads used by two major-party presidential candidates, 1960–1992	Actual turnout; / Aggregate turnout levels in nine presidential elections;	Turnout decreased with higher proportion of negative ads, **d = −.51** (although due entirely to one outlier);
	Reported turnout by 12,252 ANES respondents, 1960–1992	Actual turnout	Reported turnout was higher for survey respondents in election years with higher proportions of negative ads, **d = .01**.
9. Freedman and Goldstein 1999	Very sophisticated estimate of number of negative ads seen by survey respondents	Second wave (N = 290) of representative panel study of 1997 Virginia gubernatorial campaign / Reported turnout;	Viewing more negative ads associated with higher turnout, **d = .25**;
		Political efficacy	Exposure to negative ads slightly lowers political efficacy, **d = −.05**.

(continues)

Study	Independent Variable	Subjects and Design	Dependent Variables	Results
10. Garramone, Atkin, Pinkleton, and Cole 1990	Exposure to various combinations and numbers of positive and negative biographical profiles and political commercials for two fictional U.S. Senate candidates	Experiment with 372 students assigned to 1 of 6 conditions: control, double-positive, single-positive, negative-positive, single-negative, or double-negative	Differential affect;	Exposure to negative ads caused greater image discrimination (the difference between candidate image evaluations) than exposure to positive ads, *d* = .38;
			Voter turnout	Negative ads did not significantly affect voter turnout, *d* = −.18.
11. Geer and Lau 1998	State-based estimates of proportion of negative ads used by two major-party presidential candidates, 1960–1996	State-level turnout in ten presidential elections, 1960–1996	State-level turnout;	The higher the proportion of negative advertising used by both candidates in the state, the higher the turnout, *d* = .48;
		Reported turnout by 15,632 ANES survey respondents, 1960–1996	Reported turnout	The higher the proportion of negative advertising used by both candidates in the state, the higher the turnout, *d* = .08.

Study	Method	Outcome	Finding
12. Goldstein 1997b	Number of negative ads shown in 75 largest media markets during 1996 presidential campaign	Aggregate analysis of 1,588 counties, followed by individual-level analysis of 879 ANES respondents living in 75 largest media markets	County-level turnout;	The more negative ads run in county, the lower the turnout, **d = −.27**;
			Reported turnout;	More negative ads a respondent exposed to, greater probability of voting, **d = .09**;
			Political efficacy	More negative ads a respondent exposed to, the lower political efficacy, **d = −.05**.
13. Haddock and Zanna 1997	Impressions of actual candidates before and after controversial attack ads aired during 1993 Canadian national election	"Natural" experiment with 110 college students	Affect for sponsor of attack ads;	Affect toward sponsor of ads decreased after airing of ads, **d = −.32**;
			Affect for target of attack ads	Affect toward target of ads increased after airing of ads, **d = −.35**.
14. Hill 1989	Positive or negative ad from Bush or Dukakis campaign	Experiment with 120 college students	Affect for sponsor of attack ads;	Sponsor of ad was liked less if ad was negative rather than positive, **d = −.65**;
			Affect for target of attack ads;	Target of ad was liked more if ad was negative rather than positive, **d = −.13**;
			Affect for the ad itself	Negative ads were liked more than positive ads, **d = .73**.

(continues)

Study	Independent Variable	Subjects and Design	Dependent Variables	Results
15. Hitchon and Chang 1995	Exposure to positive, neutral, and negative ads from female and male gubernatorial candidates	Experiment using a 3 (positive, negative, neutral) $\times$ 2 (female, male) within-subject factorial design with 75 undergraduate subjects	Affect for ads;	Negative ads received more negative evaluations than positive ads, $d = -.50$;
			Affect for sponsor of attack ads;	More negative affect for candidates who attacked their opponents, $d = -.81$;
			Memory for ads	Positive ads produced highest candidate recall, while negative ads produced lowest candidate recall, $d = -.58$.
16. Hitchon, Chang, and Harris 1997	Exposure to positive, neutral, and negative ads in a gubernatorial race	Experiment using a 3 (positive, neutral, negative) $\times$ 2 (male, female) within-subject factorial design with 72 undergraduate subjects	Affect for sponsor of ads	Negative ads produced less favorable responses than positive or neutral ads, $d = .80$.
17. Kahn and Geer 1994	Actual positive or negative ads from out-of-state gubernatorial candidates inserted in regular ad breaks during a TV sitcom	Experiment with 209 college students; subjects saw one or two positive or negative ads	Affect for sponsor of ads	Sponsor of ad was liked less after one negative compared to one positive ad, $d = -.28$;
				Sponsor of ads was liked less after two negative compared to two positive ads, $d = -.74$.

Study	Design	Sample	Dependent measure	Findings
18. Kahn and Kenney 1999a	Coding of sample of campaign ads from 1988–1992 U.S. Senate elections	ANES Senate election study, $N = 2,256$	Reported turnout	Relatively greater use of negative ads by both candidates associated with higher turnout, $d = .03$.
19. Kahn and Kenney 1999b	Coding of sample of campaign ads from 1988–1992 U.S. Senate elections	ANES Senate election study, $N = 6,110$	Knowledge of Senate candidates	Respondents had more awareness of major party candidates when relatively more negative ads used, $d = .07$.
20. Kaid 1997	Exposure to actual ads from 1996 Clinton or Dole campaigns	Experiment with 116 undergraduates as subjects	Vote intention;	Subjects were much more likely to say they intended to vote for a candidate after viewing one of his negative ads compared with one positive ad, $d = 1.77$;
			Affect for target of ads;	Target of ads liked less after negative compared with positive ad, $d = .68$;
			Affect for sponsor of ads	Sponsor of negative ad liked slightly more than sponsor of positive ad, $d = .28$.
21. Kaid and Boydston 1987	One of five actual ads used by congressional candidate from another district	Convenience sample of 428 residents rated candidate before and after seeing one of his ads	Affect for target of ads	Affect for target of ads dropped after viewing negative ad, $d = .36$.

(continues)

Study	Independent Variable	Subjects and Design	Dependent Variables	Results
22. Kaid, Chanslor, and Hovind 1992	Exposure to different types of actual political ads (positive, negative, issue, image) and the type of television program surrounding the ad	Experiment with a 3 × 3 factorial design, varying program and commercial type, involving a convenience sample of 283 members of civic groups and college students	Vote intention;	Positive image ads produced greater likelihood of voting than negative ads, $d = -2.40$;
			Affect for sponsor;	Positive issue ads produced higher candidate evaluations for the sponsor than negative commercials, $d = -2.05$;
			Memory for ads	Aspects of positive issue ads were remembered more frequently than aspects of negative ads, $d = -1.15$.
23. Kaid, Leland, and Whitney 1992	Exposure to positive and negative ads from Bush and Dukakis campaigns	Experiment with 112 undergraduates who saw 3 Bush ads (2 positive, 1 negative), 3 Dukakis ads (2 positive, 1 negative), or 3 ads from both candidates (2/3 positive for each)	Memory for ads	Positive ads more likely to be remembered than expected by chance (i.e., .67), $d = -.30$.
24. King, Hendersen, and Chen 1998	Exposure to single positive or negative ad from Clinton or Dole campaigns, near end of 1996 U.S. presidential election campaign	2 × 2 × 2 experimental design using 137 undergraduates, varying positive/negative nature of ad, Clinton/Dole as sponsor of ad, and controlling on prior liking of the candidates (median split)	Liking for sponsor of ads;	Clinton liked less when exposed to his negative ad, but no effect of exposure to Dole ads, mean $d = -.32$;
			Liking for target of ads;	Dole liked less after exposure to negative Clinton ad, but no effect of exposure to Dole ads, mean $d = .31$;

			Measure	Result
			Vote intention;	Likelihood of voting for Clinton decreased after exposure to his negative ad, but no effect of exposure to Dole ads, mean $d = -.23$;
			Liking for ads;	Exposure to positive ads associated with more positive emotions and fewer negative emotions compared with exposure to negative ads in 15/18 tests, mean $d = -.51$;
			Memory for ads	Positive Clinton ads better recalled than negative Clinton ads, but no effect of exposure to Dole ads, mean $d = -.40$.
25. Lang 1991	Exposure to 8 randomly selected positive and negative ads varying emotional appeal and audiovisual format	Experiment using a 4 (order) × 2 (emotion) × 2 (format) × 4 (repetition) mixed model factorial design with 67 undergraduates	Memory for ads	More information was recalled about negative ads than positive ads, $d = .83$.

(continues)

Study	Independent Variable	Subjects and Design	Dependent Variables	Results
26. Lau, Pomper, and Mumoli 1998	Positive/negative "tone" of 1988, 1990, 1994, and 1996 U.S. Senate campaigns, coded from newspaper accounts	Ratings of both candidates by 2,686 ANES respondents and aggregate analysis of vote totals from 122 Senate elections	Differential ratings of sponsor and target of ads;	Relative liking for sponsor of ads decreased as those ads became more negative, $d = -.18$;
			Reported vote;	Relatively greater use of negative campaigning associated with fewer votes, $d = -.17$;
			Actual election outcomes;	Vote total lower than expected for candidate sponsoring more negative ads, $d = -.26$;
			Turnout	Turnout higher with relatively more negative campaigning at both the individual ($d = .06$) and aggregate level, $d = .39$.
27. Lemert, Elliot, Bernstein, Rosenberg, and Nestvold 1991	Survey respondents reflecting on a positive or negative ad they could recall seeing during 1988 presidential election	Representative sample of 1,256 respondents	Affect for sponsor of recalled ad;	Sponsor of ad was liked less if a negative ad was recalled, $d = -.34$;
			Affect for target of recalled ad;	Target of ad was liked more if a negative ad was recalled, $d = -.13$;
			Type of ad recalled	Negative ads were more likely to be recalled, $d = 3.86$.

#	Author	Independent variable	Method	Dependent variable	Results
28.	Luskin and Bratcher 1994	Authors' rating of "negativity" of 1986–1992 U.S. Senate election campaigns, based on their reading of various campaign reports	Aggregate analysis of vote totals from 125 Senate elections	Turnout	Campaign negativism decreased turnout in states with high proportion of independents ($d = -.30$) but otherwise increased turnout ($d = .27$); overall $d = -.12$.
29.	Martinez and Delegal 1990	Exposure to negative ads from one or both candidates in a hypothetical election;	Pre/post experiment with 131 college students as subjects;	Trust in government;	Trust in government increased after exposure to negative ads, $d = .14$;
		Perceived positive/negative nature of 1988 Bush and Dukakis campaigns	Representative survey of 420 respondents	Affect for sponsor of ads;	The more a candidate's campaign was perceived as negative, the less the sponsor was liked, $d = .28$;
				Affect for target of ads	The more the opposing candidate's campaign was perceived as negative, the more the target was liked, $d = -.48$.
30.	Mathews and Dietz-Uhler 1998	Exposure to positive or negative "family values" ad from mock Democratic or Republican Senate candidate	Experiment with 125 college students as subjects	Affect toward sponsor of ad;	Sponsor of positive ad liked much more than sponsor of negative ad, $d = -.52$;
				Likelihood of voting for sponsor of ad	Subjects much more likely to intend to vote for sponsor of positive ad than sponsor of negative ad, $d = -.62$.

(continues)

Study	Independent Variable	Subjects and Design	Dependent Variables	Results
31. McBride, Toburen, and Thomas 1993	Exposure to four negative ads from a 1990 Louisiana Senate race for the first experiment; exposure to a description of four negative ads from the 1992 presidential race in the second experiment	Two experiments involving 223 undergraduates from three Midwestern universities, 70 of whom were recontacted after the election to measure actual turnout	Intended turnout;	Ad valence did not significantly affect voter turnout, $d = .12$;
			Actual turnout	Controlling on race, income, interest in the campaign, and vote intention, subjects exposed to negative ads were slightly (and nonsignificantly) less likely to actually vote, $d = -.06$.
32. Merritt 1984	Exposure to negative and neutral ads from candidates in a 1982 California Assembly race	Representative survey of 314 respondents in the candidates' district	Affect toward sponsor of attack ad;	More negative affect toward sponsor when ad was negative rather than positive, $d = -.86$;
			Affect toward target of attack ad;	More negative affect toward target after negative rather than positive ad, $d = .77$;
			Correct recall of ad	Negative ad was more likely to be correctly recalled, $d = .29$.
33. Newhagen and Reeves 1991	Reactions to actual Bush and Dukakis positive, negative, or comparative ads	Within-subjects design; 30 residents reacting to 28 different ads	Memory for ads	Recall was more accurate (and quicker) for negative rather than positive ads, $d = 1.30$.

Study	Independent variable	Sample	Dependent measure	Findings
34. Pfau, Kenski, Nitz, and Sorenson 1989	Exposure to attack ad from least preferred candidate during 1988 presidential campaign, vs. no-exposure control group	Representative sample of 374 likely voters	Affect toward sponsor of ad;	Sponsor of negative ad was liked more after exposure to ad, compared with control group, $d = .75$;
			Vote intention	Respondents were more likely to intend to vote for sponsor of negative ad compared with control group, $d = .92$.
35. Pinkleton 1997	Amount of negative information about target included in ad about fictitious candidates	165 college students assigned to between-groups pre/post design (including a no-ad control group)	Affect toward sponsor of ad;	More negative the ad, less sponsor was liked, $d = -.44$;
			Affect toward target of ad;	More negative the ad, less target was liked, $d = .67$;
			Affect toward ad itself	More negative information in the ad, less it was liked, $d = -.31$.
36. Pinkleton 1998	Amount of negative information about target included in ad about fictitious candidates	165 college students assigned to between-groups pre/post design (including a no-ad control group)	Affect toward sponsor of ad;	Sponsor liked slightly less if attacks opponent, $d = -.40$;
			Affect toward target of ad;	Target liked slightly less if attacked, $d = .04$;
			Likelihood of voting for target and sponsor	Likelihood of voting for sponsor decreases slightly if attacks opponent, $d = -.03$.

(continues)

Study	Independent Variable	Subjects and Design	Dependent Variables	Results
37. Pinkleton and Garramone 1992	Number of negative ads recalled from each candidate	Phone survey of 405 likely voters just before 1990 Michigan senatorial and gubernatorial election	Intended turnout;	Intention to vote slightly higher, the more negative ads seen, $d = .01$;
			Affect for ads themselves	The more negative ads seen the less they were approved of and the less informative they were judged to be, $d = -.18$.
38. Rahn and Hirshorn 1995	Exposure to 4 positive or 4 negative ads from the 1992 election	Experiment with 53 aged 8–13 children	Public mood	Mood was lower for children exposed to 4 negative ads two years after the election, $d = -1.45$.
39. Roberts 1995	Memory for Bush or Clinton ads	Representative phone survey of 931 respondents after the 1992 presidential election	Memory for ads	Negative Bush and Clinton ads slightly more likely to be recalled than would be expected by chance, $d = .05$.
40. Roddy and Garramone 1988	Positive or negative response to opponent's attack ad	2 × 2 experiment with 274 undergraduates varying type of attack (issue or image) and nature of response (positive or negative)	Affect for sponsor of response ad;	Candidate who responded positively rather than negatively was liked more, $d = -.09$;
			Affect for target of response ad;	Target was liked less after negative response compared with positive response, $d = .06$;

Study	Manipulation	Sample/Design	Dependent variable	Results
			against sponsor of response ad;	intended to vote for candidate who responded negatively rather than positively was higher, $d = .10$;
			Affect for response ad itself	Positive response ad was liked more than negative response ad, $d = -.33$.
41. Schultz and Pancer 1997	Whether fictitious candidate attacks character of opponent	134 undergraduates randomly assigned to 2 × 2 experiment, varying sex of candidate and whether he or she attacks opponent	Affect for sponsor of attack;	No significant difference in evaluations of sponsor, (assumed) $d = 0$;
			Vote intention	No significant difference in vote intention, (assumed) $d = 0$.
42. Shapiro and Rieger 1992	Positive or negative radio ads from two fictitious candidates in two local elections	106 undergraduates in 2 × 2 mixed design: subjects heard 1 positive and 1 negative image or issue ad	Affect for sponsor of ads;	Sponsor of negative ad was liked less than sponsor of positive ad, $d = -1.89$;
			Affect for target of ads;	Target of negative ad was liked less than target of positive ad, $d = .50$;
			Vote intention;	Subjects were more likely to intend to vote for sponsor of positive ad rather than negative ad, $d = -1.29$;
			Affect toward ads themselves;	Positive ads were seen as more fair than negative ads, $d = -3.12$;
			Memory for ads	Negative ads were more likely to be remembered, $d = .54$.

(continues)

Study	Independent Variable	Subjects and Design	Dependent Variables	Results
43. Sulfaro 1998	Reported memory for positive or negative ad from 1992 and 1996 U.S. presidential campaigns	1992 and 1996 ANES surveys, $N = 4,054$	Affect for target of ads;	Negative ads increased liking of target for both low-education respondents ($d = -.02$) and high-education respondents ($d = -.01$); weighted mean $d = -.02$;
			Affect for sponsor of ads;	Affect toward sponsor of negative ad decreased for low-education ($d = -.03$) but not high-education respondents ($d = 0$); weighted mean $d = -.02$;
			Memory for ads	Negative ads recalled better than positive ads by both low-education ($d = .39$) and high-education respondents, $d = .39$;
44. Thorson, Christ, and Caywood 1991	Fictitious support or attack ads created for actual Senate candidates	161 undergraduates assigned to 2 (issue vs image) × 2 (support or attack) × 2 (presence of music) × 2 (visual background) experiment	Affect toward sponsor of ads;	Sponsor of ad was liked less if attacking, $d = -.35$;
			Vote intention;	No significant difference on vote intention, (assumed) $d = 0$;
			Affect for ads themselves;	Attack ad was liked less than support ad, $d = -.35$;

		Memory for ads	Memory was better for support than attack ad, $d = -.35$.
45. Thorson, Ognianova, Coyle, and Denton 1996	Reported exposure to positive and negative ads during the campaign	Turnout;	No significant relationship between relative exposure to positive and negative ads and reported turnout, (assumed) $d = 0$;
	Random survey of 657 residents of a northern city after gubernatorial and senatorial election	Public mood;	Exposure to negative ads was negatively related to four measures of public mood, average $d = -.30$;
		Political efficacy;	Relatively greater exposure to negative ads related to lower political efficacy, $d = -.22$;
		Trust in government;	Exposure to negative ads was negatively related to trust in government, $d = -.31$;
		Knowledge of candidates	Exposure to negative ads increased knowledge of candidates more than exposure to positive ads, $d = -.01$.

(continues)

Study	Independent Variable	Subjects and Design	Dependent Variables	Results
46. Tinkham and Weaver-Lariscy 1991	Media strategy, as reported by actual congressional candidates (positive issue, positive image, or focus on opponent)	240 responses to survey of both major-party candidates in all 333 competitive congressional races in 1982	Actual outcome (i.e., did respondent win or lose election?)	Challengers who went negative were more likely to win, $d = .14$; Incumbents who went negative were more likely to lose, $d = -.16$; Candidates in open seats who went negative were much more likely to lose, $d = -.68$; Weighted average, $\boldsymbol{d = -.10.}$*
47. Tinkham and Weaver-Lariscy 1993	Positive or negative nature of 10 actual political ads	Within-subjects design, with 201 undergraduates	Differential affect ("source utility"–"target utility")	Positive ads produced greater differential affect for sponsor of ad, $\boldsymbol{d = -4.38.}$
48. Tinkham and Weaver-Lariscy 1994	Positive or negative nature of 10 actual political ads	Within-subjects design, with 201 undergraduates	Judgments about ads themselves	7 negative ads were rated as less ethical than 3 positive ads, $\boldsymbol{d = -.87.}$
49. Wadsworth, Patterson, Kaid, Cullers, Malcomb, and Lamirand 1987	Aggressive (attack) or nonaggressive (positive) ad	Simple comparison between 44 undergraduates assigned to either condition	Affect toward sponsor of ad; Affect toward ad itself	Sponsor was liked slightly more if attacked opponent, $\boldsymbol{d = .30}$; Negative ad was liked more than positive ad, $\boldsymbol{d = 1.01.}$

50. Wattenberg and Brians 1999	Memory for positive or negative ads from the 1992 and 1996 presidential elections	Nationally representative survey of 3,216 respondents (ANES data)	Reported turnout	Negative political advertising was positively associated with voter turnout, d = .02.
51. Weaver-Lariscy and Tinkham 1996	Media strategy, as reported by actual congressional candidates (positive issue, positive image, focus on opponent, response to opponent's attacks)	295 responses to a survey of both major-party candidates in all 310 competitive congressional races in 1990	Percentage of total vote received by respondent	Controlling for incumbency, (negative) campaign strategy focusing on opponent was associated with slightly lower vote share, d = −.06.
52. Weigold 1992	Positive or negative ad by fictitious congressional candidate	116 undergraduates participating in 2 × 2 × 2 × 2 mixed factorial design	Affect for sponsor of ad; Affect for target of ad; Differential affect (sponsor–target)	Sponsor was liked less when using negative ad, d = −1.18; Target was liked less after negative ad, d = 1.90; Taken together, negative ad was more effective than positive ad, d = .72.

*For the Tinkham and Weaver-Lariscy (1991) study, the weighted average effect size was used in the meta-analysis.

Data and Methods   Appendix B

IN THIS APPENDIX, we explain the sources and methods of our analyses. Many readers, we suspect, will prefer to go directly to our findings, avoiding material that is admittedly technical and detailed. For that reason we moved most of the technical details to this appendix. For those interested in the methodological techniques, however, we here seek to provide a full explanation.

Technical Details for Meta-Analysis in Chapter 2

The studies reviewed in chapter 2 are listed in appendix A. For each study included in the meta-analysis, appendix A briefly describes the nature of the crucial independent variable; the subjects and basic design; the dependent variable(s); and the results, including our estimate of the raw effect size, d.

Locating the Studies

The first step in a meta-analysis, as in any literature review, is a comprehensive inventory of the research literature. Our starting point was the large number of political advertising studies Lau and Sigelman (1999) had accumulated over the years. To these we added articles by searching pertinent databases and documents, including *ABC Pol Sci, Communications Abstracts, Current Contents, Dissertation Abstracts, PsycINFO, Psychological Abstracts, Social Science Index, United States Political Science Documents*, and the programs for meetings of various professional associations. We also combed through the literature cited in each paper to identify additional studies that might contain pertinent findings. Our goal was to access every relevant study. We believe that we have located and analyzed the great majority of them.

Though excellent for locating published studies, these search methods are less effective for unearthing unpublished research. It is well known that published studies tend to display a bias toward overreporting statistically significant results (see, e.g., Begg 1994), so a literature review that underrepresents "fugitive" studies runs the risk of overestimating the true effects of the phenomenon in question. To minimize such bias, we (1) included in the meta-analysis pertinent unpublished convention papers and manuscripts Lau and

Sigelman had reviewed for publication and (2) then contacted the authors of studies we located, described our project, explained the need to consider *all* applicable findings (regardless of the statistical significance of the results), and requested relevant papers. In response, we received a score of new papers, several of which met our criteria for inclusion and were incorporated into the meta-analysis.

Criteria for Inclusion

Every paper, article, chapter, or book in our inventory was initially screened by one of the authors to determine whether it contained findings that met each of five criteria.

1. A focus on *negative* political advertising. We included findings in the meta-analysis only if they pertained specifically to negative political advertisements rather than generically to political advertisements without regard to valence. Recognizing that "negative advertising" is a contested concept, we based this criterion on whether the authors of a given study themselves categorized an ad as negative. Excluded by this criterion was, for example, Brians and Wattenberg's (1996) finding that those who recalled watching more campaign ads in 1992 knew significantly more about the candidates' issue positions, for that finding says nothing about the effects of *negative* ads in particular. Because the findings included in the meta-analysis were based on several different types of negative ads, we undertook a follow-up analysis, described in the latter half of chapter 2, to ascertain whether certain types of negative ads (e.g., comparative rather than pure attack ads) might be more effective and other types less so.

2. A focus on negative *political* advertising. Dozens of studies of negative *product* advertising have been undertaken (e.g., Muehling, Stoltman, and Grossbart 1990; Putrevu and Lord 1994), but we concentrated exclusively on findings concerning advertising in election campaigns.

3. A focus on negative political *advertising*. We included studies only if they contained an explicit advertising element. This criterion disqualified, for example, findings about the impact of scandals on the outcome of congressional elections (e.g., Dimock and Jacobson 1995; Welch and Hibbing 1997) and of candidate attacks in campaign debates (Roese and Sande 1993).

4. A means of gauging the *effects* of negative political advertising. This criterion eliminated studies that did not contain an outcome measure (e.g., Hale, Fox, and Farmer 1996; Kaid and Johnston 1991; West 1993). It also eliminated analyses lacking an element of comparison, because if a study focused exclusively on negative ads the possibility

could not be ruled out that the ostensible effects of these ads might hold for positive ads as well. Thus, to be included in the meta-analysis, a study had to compare negative advertisements to something else— either a "no advertisements" control group or a "positive advertisements" comparison group. This criterion eliminated some worthwhile studies of the relative effectiveness of different types of negative ads (e.g., Budesheim, Houston, and DePaola 1996; Karrh and Halpern 1997).

5. *Single counting* of a given finding. When we located nonindependent reports of the same finding (e.g., in a convention paper and in a published version of the same paper), we included only the later, and presumably more authoritative, version. By the same token, if one report included a subset of data also incorporated into a more comprehensive data set analyzed and reported upon elsewhere, we excluded the former and focused on the latter. For example, we excluded the experimentally based findings reported by Ansolabehere et al. (1994) because the 1,655 subjects on which these findings were based were a subset of the 2,216 subjects in a more comprehensive presentation that we did include (Ansolabehere and Iyengar 1995). On the other hand, a data set could provide multiple findings for the meta-analysis if more than one type of outcome measure was involved (e.g., subjects' evaluations of both the sponsor and the target of an ad).

After this screening, the senior author reexamined each excluded study to ensure that pertinent findings had not been inadvertently eliminated. Every item in the original inventory was read at least twice before being dropped from consideration.[1]

Recorded Variables

We recorded a wide array of descriptive information about the researchers and the research design associated with each finding. For present purposes, the most critical information was the operational definition of negative advertising employed by the researchers and the category into which a given outcome measure fell. Both of these issues relate to an "apples and oranges" criticism often leveled at meta-analysis. Studies made it into our review because the authors *said* their studies involved negative advertising. However, just as the actual negative (and positive) advertisements used by real candidates vary widely, so do the conceptual and operational definitions of negative advertisements used in these studies. What is the point, one might ask, of trying to summarize a diverse literature by treating findings based on different types of ads as though they were indistinguishable?

This question misses one of the greatest strengths of meta-analysis. Diversity is not a problem in meta-analysis as long as such diversity can be coded and taken into account in the analysis. In defining different types of campaign ads, the crucial factor seems to be how much negative information an ad must contain before it is called negative. Whereas some researchers treat as negative any ad that mentions the opponent, others distinguish among ads that mention only the sponsor (positive, or "advocacy" ads), ads that focus exclusively or primarily on the opponent (negative, or "attack" ads), and ads that focus on both the sponsor and the opponent ("comparative" or "contrast" ads) (Jamieson, Waldman, and Sherr 1998). We coded this information for every finding in our analysis. In our initial presentation of results, we ignore these differences, taking at face value each research team's claim to be studying negative political advertising. Subsequently we took these potentially crucial differences in definition of the independent variable into account to see whether they had any bearing on the results.[2]

The remaining data required for the meta-analysis (in addition to the effect size for each finding, as explained later) included the number of experimental subjects or survey respondents on which a given finding was based, which was easy to determine in most cases; the reliability of the outcome measure, which we had to estimate in many instances; and the strength of the political advertising "treatment" (i.e., the number and the nature of political ads to which subjects were exposed). Sample size, measurement reliability, and strength of treatment come into play when effect sizes are adjusted for sampling error, measurement error, and variation in treatment strength, as described later.

Calculating Effects

The problem of different outcome measures is resolved by calculating "effect sizes" that translate results based on different measures into a common metric. There are two major varieties of effect sizes: r measures (based on correlations) and d measures (based on mean differences). We chose the latter because most of the findings analyzed here were derived from comparisons of group means.

In the simplest case, the effect size measure is defined as follows:

$$d = (X_E - X_C)/S_x$$

That is, d, the measure of effect size, is the difference between the means of the experimental and control groups, divided by the standard deviation. Thus d is expressed in standard deviation units, closely paralleling z-scores.[3] Surprisingly often, researchers fail to report the information involved in the formula for d, even when the design of a study is as simple as a comparison between an experimental and control group. Generally, though, if even a modicum of more or less exact information (e.g., group means and an F statistic) is reported, an algebraic path can be followed to a reasonable approximation of an effect size.[4]

About a quarter of our data points come from ordinary least squares (OLS) or logistic regression equations, and there is no universally accepted method for handling such data in a meta-analysis. In general, we proceeded along two lines. The first was to ignore the magnitude of an effect and consider only its statistical significance (Becker 1994). This nonparametric "combined significance" approach is quite conservative, for it tests only the very specific null hypothesis that the effect of interest is not present in *any* of the populations studied. Second, we used the *t* value associated with a regression coefficient as a parametric estimate of the magnitude of the effect (Stanley and Jarrell 1989), and combined it with the effect sizes calculated from other studies in the analysis. This approach is much more informative about the magnitude of an effect and permits more sophisticated hypothesis tests, while considering data from all relevant studies.

Adjusting for Errors and Bias

After calculating an effect size for each finding in the meta-analysis, one has to decide how to combine them. Some experts recommend analyzing raw, "unadjusted" effect sizes, while others advocate performing a variety of adjustments prior to analysis. The underlying issue is whether to treat all studies equally. For a large and fairly homogeneous research literature, it could well be appropriate to treat all studies equally, but for a literature as diverse as the one we are considering, this would be problematic. Accordingly, we followed the adjustment guidelines established by Hunter and Schmidt (1990). In what follows we report unadjusted parametric effect sizes, followed by effect sizes adjusted first for sampling error, then for unreliability of measurement in the dependent variable, and finally for variation in the strength of the independent variable. Our conclusions were not greatly affected by these adjustments.

Most of the findings in our review involve mean differences (usually from experiments), for which the formula presented earlier for calculating *d* was used. A few come from ordinary least squares or logistic regression analyses, however, and as already noted, there are no universally accepted means of translating coefficients into effect sizes. The problem is two-fold. First, different measurement scales in the independent or dependent variables produce regression coefficients of different magnitudes. Second, even when the focal independent and dependent variables are measured on the same scale, some experts insist that regression coefficients not be compared unless all other variables in the equation are identical. In practice, this requirement is almost never met, in which case all such data must be excluded from a meta-analysis. We rejected this approach out of hand.

A second approach is to ignore the magnitude of an effect and consider only its sign and statistical significance. This nonparametric approach was actually one of the first meta-analytic techniques to find its way into the statistical literature (Fisher 1932), although it has been greatly refined since then. Becker (1994) describes several combined significance tests, of which we employ one of the simplest, converting reported significance levels to their normal (z value) equivalent (Mosteller and Bush 1954). When the null hypothesis is true, the sum of z values is normally distributed; it is divided by its standard deviation, $\sqrt{k}$, the square root of k (where k is the number of studies), and the ratio is compared with the critical values in the standard normal table.

A third approach is to devise parametric estimates of effect sizes from the regression coefficients and then combine them with the effect sizes computed from the remaining studies. Although a regression coefficient is dimensional (i.e., the measurement scales of the independent and dependent variables affect its magnitude), the t statistic associated with a regression coefficient has no such dimensionality but is a standardized measure of the effect of interest (Stanley and Jarrell 1989; see also Phillips and Goss 1995; Raju, Pappas, and Williams 1989; Kanetkar et al. 1995). Indeed, even when research designs contrast differences in means, it is often the case (when the means are not actually reported) that the effect size is calculated from a t statistic (using the standard formula $d = 2 \cdot t / \sqrt{df}$). We used that formula to calculate effect size estimates from findings presented in a regression format.

Although the statistical reasoning seems clear, it may be useful to provide an intuitive justification for this practice. In an experiment, the effects of all possible "third" variables on the dependent variable are assumed to be controlled by random assignment. In the typical research design in which some form of regression is employed, however, subjects have not been randomly assigned to conditions. Instead, the effects of possible third variables are controlled statistically by being included in the regression analysis along with the focal independent variable. As long as a regression model is reasonably well specified, we would argue, it provides a situation sufficiently similar to the typical experiment so that the effects of comparable independent variables—whether they are manipulated in an experiment or measured in a survey—can be compared across research designs.

Adjusting Estimated Effect Sizes[5]

If the population of interest is not constant across studies, the best estimate of the population effect size, Δ, is not the simple mean effect size across studies (as in table 2.1) but a weighted mean that corrects for sampling error, with weights determined by the proportion of all participants who were in a given study. Thus, our initial adjustment to effect sizes was to weight each mean by N_i/N_T, where N_i is the sample size for an individual study and N_T is the total number of participants across all studies. If D is the mean unadjusted effect size and d_i is the unadjusted effect size for each study, then D_1 is the mean adjusted effect size, controlling for the number of participants in each study. D_1 is used on the left side of table 2.2.

$$D_1 = \Sigma(N_i/N_T) \cdot d_i$$

The variance of d_1 is a weighted average squared error:

$$\text{Var}(d_1) = \Sigma(N_i/N_T) \cdot (d_1 - D_1)^2$$

However, this sample variance is a biased estimate of the population variance. To correct for this bias, the variance of the sampling error is estimated and subtracted from the sample variance. If e is the sampling error and N_a is the average sample size across studies, then

$$\text{Var}(e) = (4/N_a) \cdot (1 + D_1^2/8)$$

and the standard error is

$$\text{SD}(\delta_1) = \sqrt{\text{Var}(d_1) - \text{Var}(e)}$$

To correct for measurement unreliability, an adjusted effect size, d_1, is divided by an estimate of the square root of the measurement reliability of the outcome measure, a_i. If we call this doubly adjusted effect size d_2, then

$$d_2 = d_1/\sqrt{\alpha_i}$$

Because in practice a_i is always less than 1, $d_2 > d_1$. However, the standard error of d_2 also increases.

$$\text{SD}(\delta_2) = \text{SD}(\delta_1)/\sqrt{\alpha_i}$$

D_2, the mean of the d_2 estimates, is used in the middle panel of table 2.2.

Although we did not have information on the reliability of every outcome measure in the meta-analysis, the information we did have enhanced our confidence that missing reliabilities could safely be estimated as the average reliability within a category of outcome measures. We adopted the following convention. If reliability was not reported for a particular finding based on a multi-item outcome measure, we assigned the mean reliability of other findings within the same dependent variable category. For example, for the eight findings for which measurement reliability was reported concerning affect toward the sponsor of the ad, the mean reliability was .89. If another finding concerning affect toward the sponsor was based on a multi-item outcome measure but no reliability coefficient was reported, we assigned it a reliability of .89. However, if a finding concerning affect toward the sponsor was based on a single-item outcome measure, we set its reliability at .60, two-thirds of the mean reliability for measures in the same category, the premise being that single-item measures are generally less reliable than multi-item measures.

We attempted one additional adjustment for the data, controlling for variation in the strength of the negative advertisement "treatment" to which experimental subjects or survey respondents were exposed. Our estimate of strength of treatment involved two factors, the definition and operationalization of negative advertisements by each research team, and the number of ads to which subjects were exposed. Although we have been speaking primarily of the differences between positive ads (those that focus on the sponsor) and negative ads (those that attack the opponent), a third category is sometimes distinguished, that of contrast or comparative ads (those that explicitly mention information about at least two candidates). Some researchers devise separate experimental conditions for all three types of ads,[6] while other researchers combine contrast ads and negative ads in a single category. These three types of political advertisements might be qualitatively different (and hypothesis 1 in the text treats them as such), but they certainly are *quantitatively* different in the amount of negative information they convey about an opponent. That is, a positive ad presents no negative information about an opponent, a negative ad is composed largely of negative information about the opponent, and a contrast ad falls roughly halfway between these two extremes. Embracing this typology, we defined a "full-strength" manipulation as one contrasting negative ads with positive ads, and we treated studies that contrast positive ads with contrast ads (or with some unknown mixture of negative and contrast ads[7]) as if they were half that strength. We further refined this strength of treatment effect measure by multiplying it by the number of ads subjects were exposed to—presuming that exposure to two positive or negative ads sponsored by a candidate would have twice the effect of exposure to a single ad, and so on.[8] These adjustments are analogous to those that must be made in interpreting unstandardized regression coefficients when predictors have different ranges. The adjustment itself is simple: Each estimated effect size is divided by our estimate of treatment strength before means and standard errors are computed. These final adjusted effect sizes are reported in the last two columns of table 2.2.

Methodological Details for Analyses of Negative Campaigning

The basic subject of this book is negative campaigning. We are interested in this topic in two ways. First, we want to gauge the extent of negative campaigning and to locate the political factors that lead to its practice. This is the focus of chapter 3. In statistical terms, there we treat negative campaigning as the *dependent* variable, the effect that we try to explain. Second, we want to assess the impact of negative campaigning. This is the focus of chapters 4, 5, and 6; there we employ negative campaigning as an *independent* variable, one of many possible influences on voter turnout and on election results.

The remainder of this appendix deals with five important topics: (1) the basic data, Senate elections; (2) the measures, or variables, we developed to gauge negative campaigning; (3) three different data sets developed to study the causes and effects of negative campaigning; (4) the measures of various factors in the general campaign environment that could condition the effect of negative campaigning, and which serve as important controls in our analyses; and finally (5) issues of direction of causality or endogeneity that affect some of our crucial predictors.

Senate Elections, 1992–2002

The first chapter discussed some of the methodological advantages of considering statewide races such as Senate elections, rather than the more prominent presidential elections, for studying political campaigns. Let us reiterate one of the most important points—there are simply many more campaigns to study. The availability of multiple campaigns to examine makes this study political *science* rather than history or journalism. We are interested in the causes and effects of negative campaigning. But any complex social phenomenon has multiple causes. To distinguish between the many potential causal factors, and to be able to attribute unique causal power to any one of them, we need many more campaigns than causes in our data set.[9]

There were 208 Senate elections from 1992 through 2002, including the 200 regularly scheduled elections plus eight special elections, five occasioned by resignations and three by deaths.[10] Of those 208 elections, we exclude five races when an incumbent did not face major-party opposition (Arizona in 2000; Kansas, Massachusetts, Mississippi, and Virginia in 2002), as well as the special election to replace the disgraced Bob Packwood from Oregon in January of 1995, which occurred under extremely unusual circumstances, including an all mail-in ballot. For reasons of incomplete data explained later, we exclude another ten races. Withal, we still have a plentitude of data and quite a lot of variance—across 192 campaigns—to analyze and try to explain.

Measuring Campaign Tone

How negative is each of these candidate campaigns? To answer this central question, we develop a measure of "campaign tone."

Campaigns are not simple, in practice or in analysis. Certain important data are readily available (e.g., campaign spending in the United States) because candidates are required by law to report them. But other data—in particular, on the nature of the campaign itself—are much harder to come by. A campaign goes beyond its televised political advertisements, the most common focus of past research. Candidates engage in many activities—they give speeches, conduct rallies, distribute literature, and meet with local opinion leaders, editors, and other elites to seek endorsements (Shaw 1999). There is reason to believe that candidates are consistent across these different venues in the themes they stress (certainly their campaign managers *want* them to be consistent), but there is no guarantee that they are.

To examine the effects of the campaign more broadly, we need a more comprehensive view beyond political advertisements. We rely on estimates of the nature of the campaign gathered from newspaper accounts of the election campaigns. These accounts sometimes include descriptions of political advertisements broadcast by the different candidates, but they also include reports of a wide variety of other campaign activities.

Let us be clear that we do not argue that newspapers (rather than television) are the most important media influences on voters. We use newspapers as a reasonable record of the total conduct of campaigns. Their accounts certainly include descriptions of the political advertisements broadcast by the different candidates, but they also include reports of speeches at campaign rallies and reports of "on-the-record" conversations between media and campaign personnel. Thus in essence we are relying on the reports of a variety of different political experts (i.e., political reporters) about the nature of these campaigns. This is exactly the type of data used by Ansolabehere et al. (1994) and Franklin (1991) in their earlier research on Senate campaigns.

We coded stories about the biennial Senate elections from 1992 to 2002 that appeared in any newspaper or magazine covered by the Lexis/Nexis or Dow Jones databases during the last eight weeks of the campaigns. Our study begins with the 1992 races because that is the year databases such as Lexis/ Nexis and Dow Jones, which provide easy (searchable) access to multiple newspapers, became available. We searched in-state newspapers for articles that contained the names of both major-party candidates.[11] Our goal was to examine about forty articles per campaign, drawn from the last eight weeks of the contest. For any given week, if five or fewer articles could be found about a particular race, we coded all of them. If more than five articles were available in any week, we randomly selected five from the available articles for coding. If fewer than twenty articles could be found about any given election, we expanded our search parameters to include other regional newspapers from outside the state.

Following the guidelines provided by Franklin (1992), who had previously coded newspaper stories about the 1988 and 1990 Senate elections, we categorized each statement by one of the major-party candidates (or a representative for one of those candidates) as to whether it concerned the candidate (and was therefore positive, by our definition) or concerned the opponent (and was therefore directionally negative). These statements were further categorized as issue-based or person-based. Figure B.1 illustrates our coding scheme. Consequently we have overall measures of the proportion of statements attributed to either major-party candidate that were coded as negative, and separate measures of the proportion of issue-based statements and person-based statements that were negative.

All told, we collected and read 6,365 newspaper articles about the 202 competitive Senate elections between 1992 and 2002. These stories included just over 22,000 direct quotes from the candidates or their spokespersons, an average of about 32 stories and 109 codable comments per election campaign. We set a minimum standard of 16 articles and 32 codable statements before a campaign could be included in our data set. By these criteria, we could not find enough newspaper stories about the campaign for nine elections (Louisiana and Vermont in 1992, Hawaii and Mississippi in 1994, Mississippi in 1996, Alaska and Hawaii in 1998, Hawaii in 2000, and Alaska in 2002) to have any confidence we were measuring the true nature of the campaign. Fortunately, none of these races were at all competitive. We also excluded the 1998 election in Vermont, although we had a goodly number of articles about the campaign, because it simply did not fit our coding

Figure B.1   Examples of Campaign Tone Coding

	Positive	Negative
Issue- or Record-Based Statements	"I don't want [tax] deductions because I don't want the IRS."	"Senator Murray's record has been rated as the most liberal in the entire Senate."
	"We have to require higher standards, reduce class size, replace portables with real classrooms, and restore discipline."	"In fact, Smith voted to cut Medicare $270 billion. Smith also voted to freeze Medicare to pay for big corporate tax cuts. Smith even voted to eliminate nursing home standards that protect our most vulnerable seniors."
Person-Based Statements	"Here is a woman standing on principle. They understand it totally." "I am focused on issues the people want."	"The only thing she won on before was being a woman with tennis shoes." "We find this to be the ultimate hypocrisy for a candidate who has said she wouldn't take special interest money."

Note: In each cell above, the first quote comes from Linda Smith, Republican challenger for the 1998 Senate seat in Washington, while the second quote comes from the campaign of Democratic incumbent Patty Murray. These statements are fairly representative, and the categorization of most of them is obvious. The second example in the positive person-based cell fits into this category (even though "issues" are mentioned) because the candidate is arguing that she is empathic, or "one of the people," rather than talking about any specific issue. The first example in the negative person-based cell is placed in that category because the candidate is challenging the personal qualifications of her opponent for the job.

scheme.[12] This leaves us with measures of the nature of the major-party candidates' campaigns for 192 Senate elections.

Our data are thus different from measures based strictly on the political advertisements broadcast by a candidate, which should more properly be called "advertising tone" (Finkel and Geer 1998; Kahn and Kenney 1999a), although we would expect the two measures to be positively correlated. Similarly, our data differ from Kahn and Kenney's (1999a) tone of the news coverage because we ignore statements coming from the author of the article, limiting our coding to statements coming from spokespersons for either major-party candidate. We would agree that our measure of the nature of the campaign is not ideal; good data of that nature are simply very hard to come by, particularly over such a long time period and so many distinct campaigns. No one, in the research we have seen, has what we would consider "ideal" data on the nature of a large number of campaigns. The real question is, are our data reasonable estimates of the nature of these many Senate campaigns?

Figure 3.1, in the main text of this book, presents the basic campaign tone data. The figure illustrates the overall rate of campaign negativism across election years, along with the percent of negative issue-based and person-based statements. Several points are immediately obvious from this figure. The impression the casual observer would get from reading popular accounts of recent U.S. elections is that they are all little more than "30 second snarls" (Will 1994). According to our data, however, which systematically look at those races, that characterization is just wrong. The overall level of campaign negativism across the six most recent election years is just over one third. The mean level of issue-based negativism is even lower—under 29 percent, on average. The mean level of person-based negativism is considerably higher, however (averaging 53 percent across election years), particularly before 1998, but person-based statements make up a relatively small proportion of all statements coming from the candidates, so the overall figures are always much closer to the issue-based figures.

One major caveat should be mentioned about these data. It is very possible that the press, at least in recent years, exaggerates the degree of negativism in campaigns (Capella and Jamieson 1997; Lichter and Noyes 1996; Patterson 1994; Sabato 1993). Negative campaigning, mudslinging, and so on are common ways that stories about campaigns are "framed." Following this line of reasoning, our data may better reflect how the campaign was *reported* than how it was actually *conducted*.

We certainly accept the idea that the media probably exaggerate the amount of campaign negativism. Thus we must be very careful in interpreting the absolute *level* of negative campaigning identified in our data. But we do not accept this criticism as a major threat to our data's general validity. First, most candidates are very aware of reporting biases in the media and do everything they can to take advantage of them. How the media cover a campaign certainly influences what candidates actually do, and the message that media-savvy candidates *intend* to send may well take these reporting biases into account. Thus there may be less of a disparity between what candidates intend and what the media report than between what the candidates do and what is reported.

Second, we understand why overall levels of campaign negativism might be exaggerated by the media, and there is evidence that the media exaggerate how negative political campaigns actually are (Kaid, Tedesco, and McKinnon 1996). We might therefore want to somewhat discount the *level* of negative campaigning revealed in our data. But unless this bias works differently for coverage of the incumbents, challengers, and open-seat candidates, it should not affect our conclusions. We can think of no reason why such exaggerations should systematically distort the *distribution* of campaign tone among candidates or across campaigns.

Third, the campaign as reported by the media, while not identical to the campaign conducted by the candidates, is nevertheless in no small part the campaign that is *experienced by the public*. We agree that our measure of the nature of the campaign is not ideal; unfortunately, good evidence on the nature of political campaigns is simply very hard to come by, particularly when looking at multiple campaigns in multiple locations across different election years.

It is possible that our measure of the campaign's tone, based on a coding of secondary reports from a variety of political experts in each state, is too gross or indirect or noisy to accurately reflect the true nature of each candidate's campaign. We do not believe such criticism is justified. In chapter 3, we examine seven factors that theoretically *should* be associated with the use of negative campaigning by political candidates; we find empirical support for each of those seven hypothesized factors, at least at the level of zero-order associations. Although our primary concern in chapter 3 is more substantive, these results can be viewed as providing strong *construct validity* for our measure of campaign tone.[13]

Three Distinct Data Sets

The different goals of our analysis—and good science—necessitate bringing multiple data sets to bear on our primary questions. Our primary data set has a Senate election as the unit of analysis and covers 192 usable cases drawn from the 208 elections between 1992 and 2002, one for each included Senate election in this period. This data set begins with very basic and readily available information about each Senate election, including the Democratic and Republican candidates running in each election, which candidate (if either) was the incumbent and how many prior terms he or she had served, how many votes each candidate received plus how many votes any third-party candidates received, how much money they had to spend, and so on. We relied on the biennial *Almanac of American Politics* (e.g., Barone, Cohen, and Ujifusa 2003) for this information. We also recorded standard demographic information about each state found in the *Almanac*, such as the percentage of state residents over age sixty-five, the percentage nonwhite, the percentage with a college education, and so on.

To this standard information we added our measures of the tone of each candidate's campaign, as described earlier; measures of the quality of challenger and open-seat candidates, plus indicators of incumbent weaknesses, to be described later; basic political variables about the state, such as its partisan and ideological nature (Wright, Erikson, and McIver 1985) and a state "culture" of voter turnout (again, all described more thoroughly later in the appendix); and indicators of the media consultant and pollster who worked for each candidate. We use this aggregate state-level data set in our analyses of turnout and of the effectiveness of negative campaigning.

One could argue, however, that an aggregate-level analysis of an individual decision is misspecified. A more definitive test of the effects and effectiveness of negative campaigning on turnout and the vote decision can be provided by individual-level data, using surveys conducted by the American National Election Studies. Here the individual voter is the unit of analysis (or rather, the individual citizen, as many of them don't vote). We selected respondents from states with a Senate election from the surveys conducted in 1992 through 2002 and combined the various surveys into a single individual-level data set with 6,531 respondents. Of the 208 Senate elections over this period, 156 are represented in the survey data. We then combined with the survey data relevant information from our aggregate data set about the candidates and their campaigns, producing a "cross-level" data set including both aggregate and individual-level measures.

Neither of these two data sets is appropriate for questions about who uses negative campaigning, however. For such questions the unit of analysis must be the candidate rather than the campaign or the citizen. Thus we took our basic state-level data set and split it in half, so that first the Democrat is the principal candidate of interest and the Republican is the opponent, and then the Republican is the candidate of interest and the Democrat is the opponent. Thus all candidates appear in this data set at least twice, once as a "candidate" and once as an "opponent." Some individuals—incumbents running for reelection twice during our time frame—appear twice as "candidates," although in such cases their "opponents" were always different.[14] The *N* for this data set, once we eliminate noncompetitive races and states with too few newspaper stories to reliably measure the nature of the campaign, is 384.

Control Variables

Our measure of a campaign's tone, the primary focus of this book, has already been described. We wish to see the campaign's influence on turnout and the outcome of the election. But we cannot look at the effects of this one variable in isolation, of course, because it does not operate in isolation. Both turnout and the vote choice have been widely studied in political science, and their multiple determinants are fairly well known. We need to consider the effects of campaign tone in a well-specified equation that controls for all of these other known determinants. In this section we will describe all of the control variables used in our various analyses. Most of them are well known to researchers in this area and require nothing but the briefest descriptions. But several of these variables have been built specifically for this study and therefore deserve somewhat more elaborate descriptions.

The following variables, all measured at the state level, serve as controls in our aggregate-level analyses.

Expected vote outcome represents what candidates reasonably "expected" to happen in the election when they devised their campaign strategy. To estimate those expectations, we regressed the actual outcome of the election (Republican percentage of the two-party vote) on three variables: which, if any, candidate was the incumbent; the average (or "normal") percentage vote received by the Republican candidate in the past three Senate races in the state; and the annual changes in per capita disposable income in the state (the economic indicator which seems to have the strongest effect on political outcomes). As shown in table B.1, these three variables, all of which are known well before the election, do an excellent job of predicting the vote outcome. The predicted scores from this regression serve as our measure of the expected outcome of the election.

Expected closeness of the race could affect not only turnout (many people do not bother to vote if they believe the race will be one-sided, but they do go to the polls if the election appears close) but also choice of campaign strategy. Most previous researchers who employed closeness of the race as a predictor have simply employed the actual observed closeness as that variable. But such a measure clearly cannot be known *before* the election itself. Instead, we rely on our expected vote outcome variable just described. The expected

Table B.1   Modeling Candidate Expectations: Republican Percentage of Two-Party Vote

	B	S.E.
Incumbent Senator (Republican)	9.04***	.76
Normal Senate Vote (% Republican) in State	.35***	.06
% Change in Per Capita Disposable Income	.82*	.37
Constant	36.99***	3.60
Adjusted R^2	.58	
Standard Error	8.63	

*$p < .05$ ***$p < .001$
Note: $N = 202$.

closeness of the race is the absolute value of the expected vote outcome, minus 50. We then reverse this variable so that "close" elections are scored high. All else equal, this variable should be positively related to turnout.

Relative campaign spending is the percentage, of all money spent by the major-party candidates, that was spent by the Democrat (or the Republican) alone.

Voting-age population represents the number of adult citizens living in each state, as estimated by the Census Bureau. If citizens of more populated states are more alienated or estranged from their representatives, or otherwise face higher costs in voting, this variable will be negatively related to turnout.

Campaign intensity is defined as the natural log of per capita total campaign spending by both major candidates together. All spending figures are expressed in constant 1988 dollars. Campaign intensity should be positively related to turnout.

State turnout culture measures the average turnout in the state from the three prior *presidential* elections. This was computed as a "sliding" average, so that in 1992 it is based on turnout from the 1980, 1984, and 1988 presidential elections, while in 1994 and 1996 it is based on turnout from the 1984, 1988, and 1992 presidential elections, and so on. It should be positively related to turnout.

Presidential election year is a dummy variable that equals +1 in 1992, 1996, and 2000 and is zero in all remaining years. This variable should be positively related to turnout, as it is well known that many more people vote when there is a presidential election on the ballot.

Governor's election year is a dummy variable that equals +1 when there is the added stimulation of a gubernatorial election on the ballot; it is zero otherwise. Most states hold their gubernatorial elections in off years, when there is no presidential election. But a decent minority of states hold their gubernatorial elections at the same time as the presidential election, and a handful of states hold their gubernatorial elections in odd-numbered years. This variable should be positively related to turnout, all else equal.

South is a dummy variable that equals +1 for Alabama, Arkansas, Florida, Georgia, Louisiana, Mississippi, North Carolina, South Carolina, Texas, and Virginia and is zero otherwise. Turnout has sometimes been found to be lower in southern states; if so, this variable will be negatively related to turnout.

Percent over sixty-five, percent college educated, percent rural, and percent white are all based on census figures. Age, education, place of residence, and race have all been positively related to turnout, and each of these four variables should likewise be positively related to turnout, all else equal.

Presidential popularity indicates the average approval rating of the president from all Gallup polls conducted during July, August, and September of the election year. After subtracting 50 for computational ease, this variable is multiplied by −1 if the Senate candidate is of a different party than the incumbent president. If popular presidents help candidates from their own party (i.e., if Senate elections are in part referenda on the president's job performance), this variable will be positively related to vote for an incumbent or open-seat candidate of the president's party.

Midterm election reflects the normal loss of seats by the president's party in off years. In incumbent races, it equals + 1 when a candidate of the president's party is seeking reelection during an off year, equals −1 if a candidate from the opposite party is seeking reelection, and is zero otherwise. In open-seat contests in off years, it equals + 1 in 2002 when there was a Republican president, −1 in 1994 and 1998 when the president was a Democrat, and is zero in presidential election years. This variable should be negatively related to vote for the incumbent or the Republican candidate in open-seat races.

State partisanship represents the percentage of people in the state who identify with the incumbent's party, minus the percent who identify with the other party. This variable should be positively related to vote percent for the incumbent or the candidate of the president's party.[15]

Change in state per capita disposable income (PCDI) is reported by the Bureau of Economic Activity. This objective indicator of the nature of the state's economy should be positively related to vote for the incumbent, assuming citizens are more likely to support incumbents when economic times are good but are more likely to prefer a change in their political leaders (irrespective of party) when economic times are bad.

Incumbent characteristics include three dummy variables for races involving incumbents: *scandal*, *controversy*, and *health*. These variables indicate if the incumbent had been involved in a potentially illegal scandal or an equally damning (but not illegal) controversy, or if the incumbent's ability to perform the job had been questioned for health reasons. These data were coded by reading the preelection issue of *Congressional Quarterly* each year.[16] Although these three distinct dummy variables have too little variance to possess much power in any statistical analysis, we retained them all to maintain some continuity with past research. Each of these variables should be negatively related to percent vote received by the incumbent. They are not relevant to open-seat races.

Challenger quality is measured by four dummy variables indicating the quality of the candidate. Each variable equals + 1 if it describes the challenger and equals zero otherwise. The specific variables follow:

Governor, indicating whether the candidate was the current or recently retired governor of the state;

Major office holder, indicating whether the candidate held some lesser statewide office (e.g., lieutenant governor) or was the mayor of a major city in the state;

House, indicating whether the candidate was a member of the House of Representatives;

Minor office holder, indicating whether the challenger was the mayor of a small town or city, was a state legislator, or held some other relatively minor elective office.

The "excluded category" would be candidates with no prior electoral history, who would be scored zero on all four of these variables.

Democratic and Republican candidate quality is based on the same set of indicators as challenger quality, except collapsed into a single variable for each candidate in open-seat races to save degrees of freedom for the analysis. If open-seat candidates were current or recent governors, they are given a score of $+3$; if they held some other major statewide position or were in the House of Representatives, they are given a score of $+2$; if they held some minor elective office, they are given a score of $+1$; otherwise they are given a score of zero.

The range and mean of all state-level variables are shown in table B.2.

The following control variables were used in the individual-level survey analyses.

Party identification and *ideological identification*, the two familiar 7-point scales, with respondents claiming no such identification placed at the midpoint of each scale. These variables were coded such that Republican and conservative identifiers are scored high when there was a Republican incumbent senator or open-seat races, while Democratic and liberal identifications are scored high when the incumbent is a Democrat. Each variable should predict positively to vote for the incumbent or the Republican.

Strength of partisanship reflects the relative commitment to the two major parties. This variable takes the standard measure of party identification and "folds" it at its midpoint such that pure independents are low and strong partisans are high. This variable should be positively related to turnout.

Policy preferences represents a count of the number of different government programs for which respondents wanted more spending, subtracted from the number of programs for which respondents wanted less spending. This variable was reversed whenever there was a Democratic incumbent so that it should predict positively in all elections.

Approval of the president's job performance, the standard item, with respondents who answer "Don't know" placed at the middle of the scale. Approval is scored high when the incumbent president is a Republican, low when he is a Democrat, but is reversed whenever the incumbent senator is from a different party than the president. This variable should be positively related to voting for the incumbent and the Republican.

National economy better, the standard retrospective judgment, with respondents who answer "Don't know" placed at the middle ("Stayed about

Table B.2 Variable Means and Ranges for Aggregate-Level Data

	Low	High	Mean
Variables Available for All Analyses (N = 202)			
Expected Closeness of Race	0.0	20.51	11.60
Presidential Election Year	0.0	1.0	.51
Governor's Election Year	0.0	1.0	.47
Voting-Age Population (Millions)	.34	24.62	4.54
South	0.0	1.0	.19
Percent College Educated	14.4	41.4	24.4
Percent Rural	4.5	66.8	29.5
Percent over 65	4.4	18.2	12.5
Percent White	24.3	98.2	80.9
State Turnout Culture	40.0	68.5	54.3
Presidential Popularity	−15.0	17.0	3.3
State Partisanship	−34.0	20.0	−10.6
State Change in PCDI	−.5	9.8	4.6
Variables Available for Incumbent vs. Challenger Races (N = 141)			
Incumbent Vote Percent	39.0	88.1	59.7
Expected Incumbent Vote	51.4	68.5	60.5
Midterm Election	−1.0	1.0	.01
Incumbent Scandal	0.0	1.0	.03
Incumbent Controversy	0.0	1.0	.12
Incumbent Health Problems	0.0	1.0	.03
Challenger a Governor	0.0	3.0	.04
Challenger Major Office Holder	0.0	3.0	.17
Challenger in House	0.0	3.0	.16
Challenger Minor Office Holder	0.0	3.0	.21
Incumbent Spending per Capita	.11	2.15	.86
Challenger Spending per Capita	0.0	2.77	.47
Incumbent Negativism	0.0	72.2	29.7
Challenger Negativism	0.0	84.4	41.4
Variables Available for Open-Seat Races (N = 49)			
Republican Vote Percent	35.3	71.0	51.9
Predicted Republican Percent	42.4	58.4	51.1
Democratic Candidate Quality	0.0	3.0	1.53
Republican Candidate Quality	0.0	3.0	1.55
Democratic Spending per Capita	.17	2.05	.63
Republican Spending per Capita	.10	1.54	.67
Democratic Negativism	6.1	59.8	37.5
Republican Negativism	7.7	85.7	41.4

the same") of the scale. "Better" is scored high when the senatorial candidate is of the same party as the president, and scored low when the candidate is of the opposite party. This variable should predict positively.

Campaign exposure is a combination of two separate variables, the familiar "campaign interest" item and a scale measuring media exposure, constructed by averaging items reflecting how closely the respondent followed politics on television and in the newspapers.

The individual-level analysis also includes standard demographic controls for age, education, income, race (nonwhite), gender, marital status, time in the community, and home ownership, measured at the individual level.

Questions of Direction of Causality and Endogeneity

We cannot evaluate the impact of negative campaigning in isolation. Campaigns take place in a strategic environment conditioned by candidate expectations and candidate interactions. Campaign strategies are not devised in a vacuum, of course. Candidates begin their campaigns with some, often extensive, knowledge of the likely outcome of the election and of the likely conduct of their opponents. These expectations make it easier or more difficult for candidates to raise money, and they can lead the strongest possible challengers to jump into the race or decide not to run. This means that, to some extent, campaigns are *endogenous*—interactively related—to the likely outcome of the election itself, a severe problem when we want to use campaign variables as *predictors* of election outcomes.

The problems with treating some critical variables (e.g., candidate spending) as if they were exogenous (i.e., not themselves influenced by the dependent variable) are well known in the literature (Abramowitz 1988; Gerber 1998; Green and Krasno 1988; Jacobson 1978). The analytic problem, as all participants in this debate recognize, is that campaign spending is essentially a function of the expected election outcome, which is generally very closely related to the outcome of the election itself. When an incumbent seems particularly vulnerable, it will be easier for challengers to raise money, and incumbents will typically face high-quality, well-financed opponents. Electoral success will be positively correlated with challenger spending. But this simple equation works in just the opposite fashion for incumbents. If the election looks close, supporters will be particularly likely to contribute to the incumbent; but if the election looks like a landslide, the incumbent will cut back on fund-raising activities, generating a negative correlation between likely electoral success and incumbent spending. In technical terms, this is known as endogeneity in the spending equations.

Campaign strategies are equally problematic. They are not chosen randomly, nor are they devised without any knowledge of the likely outcome of the election (Haynes and Rhine 1998). To begin with, we certainly assume that candidates generally choose the campaign strategy they believe will give them the best chance of winning the election, although there will inevitably be a great deal of uncertainty associated with this choice. At the outset of the campaign, candidates who expect to lose may attack their opponents out of desperation, or because they feel they have "nothing to lose." Candidates with less money to spend than their opponents may go negative because they believe they get "more bang for the buck" with such a strategy. Chapter 3 provides some empirical backing for these speculations.

If we ignore the problem of endogeneity, we get strange results. One of the early findings in the candidate spending literature is that spending by the challenger matters, but spending by the incumbent is irrelevant to electoral success. No incumbents that we have observed act as if they believe that. The findings for negative campaigning are equally bizarre. Using our aggregate data, we regressed the percentage of the two-party vote received by the Republican candidate on a simple measure of the *relative* use of negative campaigning by the two candidates. If life were simple and going negative an effective campaign strategy, as many practitioners seem to believe, then the more negative candidate should get more votes, and our measure of the relative negativism of the two campaigns should be positively associated with election outcome. In fact, the coefficient is negative, a whopping $-.30$ (S.E. $= .03$; adjusted $R^2 = .39$). Either going negative is a horribly ineffective campaign strategy, or something else is going on.

That "something else," most obviously, is that almost all candidates have a reasonably accurate sense of how likely they are to win well before the campaign begins. What we are seeing in the $-.30$ association is, to some degree, that candidates who expect to lose, no matter how they campaign, disproportionately choose to attack their opponents.[17]

The general problem, in a statistical sense, is that the unmeasured or unexplained portions of the dependent variable (election outcomes) are related to unmeasured or unexplained portions of the troubling independent variables (e.g., spending, campaign tone), and this violates one of the basic assumptions of different types of regression analyses, which is that the predictors are unrelated to the errors or unexplained portions of the equation. The solution to this problem is to try to find variables ("instruments") that are related to the independent variable(s) that is causing problems but are *not* related to the dependent variable of interest—in our case, the outcome of the election. These instruments are then used, along with all the other predictors in the equation of interest, in a "first-stage" regression to predict the independent variable that is causing the problem. The predicted scores from this first equation are consequently "purged" of any correlation with unmeasured aspects of the dependent variable, and the statistical conundrum is solved.

The predicted scores from the first-stage equation are then used in place of the problematic variable in a "second-stage" regression.

The analyses in chapters 3, 4, and 5 all face this problem of endogeneity. In chapter 3 we want to explain why candidates decide to go negative, but one of our important predictor variables is the tone of the opponent's campaign. These two variables clearly influence each other simultaneously or reciprocally—but then we cannot correctly use one of them as a predictor of the other. We therefore turn to two-stage least squares (2SLS). As possible instruments, we have three variables available to us: the tone of the campaign by the opponent's party candidate in the last election for this same Senate seat (six years ago, in normal circumstances) to pick up state norms, and dummy variables representing Mid-Atlantic and Plains states, to pick up regional norms.

The first-stage regression is shown in table B.3. Following Bartels's (1991) recommendations, the table lists the explained variance (R^2) from three separate equations, the first from the full purging regression presented in the table, the second when only the exogenous variables from the second-stage regression are used as independent variables, and the last when the predicted score from the first-stage equation is itself regressed on those same

Table B.3   First-Stage Regressions Predicting Use of Negative Campaigning by Opposing Candidate

	B	S.E.
Instruments		
Use of Negative Campaigning by Opposite Party Candidate in Last Senate Election in State	.07	.06
Mid-Atlantic State	6.56*	2.97
Plains State	3.10	2.26
Exogenous Predictors		
Expected Vote Outcome	.17	.23
Expected Closeness of Race	.84***	.25
Relative Campaign Spending	.13**	.05
Challenger	−2.69	5.13
Open Seat	−4.24	3.68
Party (Republican)	−4.34**	1.65
Female Candidate	−3.35	2.34
Constant	22.03	13.90
R^2 Full Purging Equation	.24	
R^2 Just Exogenous Variables	.22	
R^2 Predicted Score Regressed on Exogenous Variables	.93	

*$p < .05$ **$p < .01$ ***$p < .001$
Note: Table entries are unstandardized OLS coefficients. $N = 382$.

exogenous variables. In this appendix we want to briefly explain what we should be looking for in these first-stage analyses. Most obviously, for a "good" first-stage regression you want a model that explains a lot of variance in the first-stage dependent variable. We are going to substitute the predicted scores from this analysis for that variable when it is used as a predictor in the second-stage regression, and if we cannot predict very much of the variance in the first-stage regression, we are fooling ourselves if we think we have resolved any of the sticky statistical issues. As a rule of thumb, an R^2 from this initial "full purging equation" of .20 might be considered a minimally acceptable value. All of our first-stage models exceed this minimal value.

But a relatively large R^2 from the initial regression is not enough. It must also be the case that a good deal of the "explaining" is being accomplished by the instrumental variables, rather than by the exogenous variables (the remaining predictors from the second-stage regression, about which there are no doubts of direction of causality). Thus each of our tables includes a second R^2 value, this one from a regression (not shown in any table) where the only predictors were the exogenous variables listed in each table. If this second R^2 value is nearly as large as the first (it cannot be larger), most of the explaining in the first-stage regression is being accomplished by the exogenous variables rather than the instruments, and the instruments are adding no new information to the mix. This is the problem in table B.3, where the R^2 from the second equation (.22) is nearly as large as the R^2 from the first (.24). We have therefore been able to add little new information; as a consequence, our second-stage predictor is weak. In all of the remaining first-stage regressions, however, anywhere from a third to well over two-thirds of the explainable variance is being explained by the instruments, and as a consequence we have very good second-stage predictors.

As a final indication of how much independent information the first-stage predicted scores can bring to the second-stage regression, we regress them on the exogenous predictors from the first-stage regression. If the R^2 from this subsidiary regression is close to 1, as it is in table B.3 (.93), there is very little unique information in the predicted score (i.e., information that is not shared by one of the exogenous variables in the equation), and it cannot have much power in the second-stage regression. Once again, only the analysis in table B.3 proves problematic.

We employed four instruments for incumbent spending: the total amount spent by both candidates in the previous Senate election in the state (which should be positively related to current spending), the voting age population of the state (negatively related to spending), and dummy variables indicating whether the incumbent was a member of the Finance Committee (Romer and Snyder 1994) or was the chair of Budget, Commerce, or Finance committees or the majority leader. For challenger spending, we employed three instruments: total lagged spending, voting-age population, and a dummy variable indicating whether the incumbent was rich (Gerber 1998). These results are shown in table B.4. The first-stage regression for incumbent spending is excellent; for challenger spending, it is more than acceptable.

We considered a number of variables as possible first-stage instruments for campaign tone, including the tone of the incumbent's campaign the last time this seat was up for election (usually six years ago), the projected closeness of the race, and dummy variables for region, party, candidate gender, election year, and the polling firm and media consultant working for each candidate.[18] To avoid "over fitting," we retained only those possible predictor variables with coefficients approximately as large as (or larger than) their standard errors. These results are shown in table B.5. As with spending, we estimated separate first-stage regressions for incumbents and challengers. Both of these equations provided very good first-stage estimates of the campaign's tone.

Finally, the first-stage regressions for open-seat Democrats' and Republi-

Table B.4   First-Stage Regressions for Candidate Spending

	Incumbent		Challenger	
	B	S.E.	B	S.E.
Instruments				
Lagged Total Spending	.19***	.03	.19**	.07
Voting-Age Population	−.001***	.000	−.001	.000
Incumbent on Finance Comm.	.26*	.11		
Incumbent Committee Chair	.13	.19		
Challenger Rich			1.03**	.33
Exogenous Predictors				
Presidential Popularity	−.00	.01	−.01	.01
Midterm Election	.09	.06	.33*	.16
State Partisanship	1.19**	.35	1.76@	.93
State Change in PCDI	−.03	.03	−.04	.07
Incumbent Scandal	−.15	.27	.20	.72
Incumbent Controversy	.27*	.13	1.21***	.36
Incumbent Health Problems	−.19	.28	.83	.73
Challenger a Governor	.47@	.25	1.83**	.65
Challenger Major Office	.14	.12	1.19***	.33
Challenger in House	.34**	.13	1.75***	.35
Challenger Minor Office	.02	.11	.40	.30
Constant	.19	.17	−2.05***	.45
R^2 Full Purging Equation	.62		.37	
R^2 Just Exogenous Variables	.17		.27	
R^2 Predicted Score Regressed on Exogenous Variables	.27		.72	

@ $p < .10$ * $p < .05$ ** $p < .01$ *** $p < .001$
Note: N = 153.

Table B.5   First-Stage Regressions for Campaign Negativism

	Incumbent		Challenger	
	B	S.E.	B	S.E.
Instruments				
Lagged Campaign Tone	.20*	.10	.07	.10
Projected Closeness of Race	82*	.41	−.33	.40
Female Candidate	−.69	5.24	−1.91	4.05
Candidate's Party (Republican)	3.55*	1.52	−1.77	1.52
Democratic Media Consultant 1	7.18*	3.67		
Democratic Media Consultant 2	−23.14**	8.29	−8.35	8.04
Republican Media Consultant 1	11.59*	4.70		
Republican Media Consultant 2	13.89*	6.82	−8.70	7.18
Republican Media Consultant 3	2.43	7.41		
Republican Media Consultant 4			11.05@	6.62
Democratic Pollster 1	8.39**	3.26		
Republican Pollster 1	18.28**	7.07	18.99**	7.47
Republican Pollster 2	5.41	5.50	7.05	4.87
Republican Pollster 3	16.22**	5.85	10.48@	5.83
Republican Pollster 4			8.53	6.11
Republican Pollster 5			5.62	4.11
Republican Pollster 6			19.44**	7.51
Republican Pollster 7			10.61@	6.05
Republican Pollster 8			13.05*	5.44
Northeast State			8.07@	4.31
Mid-Atlantic State	11.76*	4.95		
Plains State			3.29	4.30
West Coast State	7.43	5.85		
Exogenous Variables				
Midterm Election	5.82**	1.99	4.42*	1.90
State Partisanship	25.50*	11.71	28.29*	12.29
State Change in PCDI	.15	1.03	−1.25	1.05
Incumbent Scandal	15.18@	8.68	5.40	7.91
Incumbent Controversy	14.85***	4.32	5.53	4.31
Incumbent Health Problems	−2.14	8.32	.73	8.11
Challenger a Governor	17.46*	7.78	2.59	7.93
Challenger Major Office	3.07	3.89	8.75*	3.95
Challenger in House	7.78@	4.19	8.11*	4.09
Challenger Minor Office	−2.56	3.57	−.23	3.52
Constant	15.50	8.06	44.02***	7.43
R^2 Full Purging Equation	.50		.45	
R^2 Just Exogenous Variables	.24		.22	
R^2 Instrument Regressed on Exogenous Variables	.48		.49	

@$p < .10$ *$p < .05$ **$p < .01$ ***$p < .001$
Note: Equations also include year dummies. $N = 142$.

cans' spending and campaign tone are shown in tables B.6 and B.7. For spending, we use as instruments spending by the party's candidate from the prior election for this same Senate seat, the state's voting-age population, and a dummy variable indicating whether the candidate was rich. For campaign tone, we use as instruments the tone of the party's candidate from the last time this same Senate seat was up for election and dummy variables for region, election year, and media consultant and pollster. These first-stage regressions all varied between acceptable and very good.

This completes our description of the different data sets we analyze in the book, the primary variables in our analysis, and most important, our measurement of the campaign's tone. We also discussed some fairly complicated issues of direction of causality and described our means of handling them. Bartels (1991) provides an excellent summary of these issues.

Table B.6   First-Stage Regressions for Candidate Spending, Open-Seat Races

	Democrat		Republican	
	B	S.E.	B	S.E.
Instruments				
Lagged Spending	−.10	.11	.31*	.13
Voting-Age Population	−.001*	.000	−.001	.000
Candidate Rich	.05	.39	.20	.29
Exogenous Predictors				
Candidate Governor	.44	.37	−.43	.35
Candidate Major Office	−.39	.36	−.23	.28
Candidate in House	−.14	.30	−.17	.27
Candidate Minor Office	−.84@	.44	−.80**	.29
Presidential Popularity	−.01	.01	.01	.01
Normal Vote	.01	.02	−.00	.01
State Partisanship	−.63	1.37	−.08	.91
State Change in PCDI	.11	.08	−.08	.06
Constant	−.56	.63	.58	.55
R^2 Full Purging Equation	.35		.55	
R^2 Just Exogenous Variables	.24		.21	
R^2 Instrument Regressed on Exogenous Variables	.68		.38	

@$p < .10$ *$p < .05$ **$p < .01$
Note: $N = 49$.

Table B.7   First-Stage Regressions for Candidate Negativism, Open-Seat Races

	Democrat		Republican	
	B	S.E.	B	S.E.
Instruments				
Lagged Campaign Tone	−.13	.11	.16	.13
Democratic Media Consultant 1	7.30	5.51		
Democratic Media Consultant 3	−7.42	5.69		
Democratic Media Consultant 4	8.39	6.12		
Democratic Pollster 2	2.52	5.01		
Republican Media Consultant 5			−9.79*	4.42
Republican Pollster 1			8.97	7.51
Mountain State	5.44	5.48		
Upper Midwest State			−5.71	6.97
1994 Election			10.52	6.58
1998 Election	−18.84**	6.45	−9.96	7.38
Exogenous Predictors				
Candidate Governor	−4.38	6.17	−.73	8.27
Candidate Major Office	−1.98	5.61	14.60*	6.54
Candidate in House	2.26	4.75	3.38	5.45
Candidate Minor Office	3.20	7.36	−5.30	7.10
Presidential Popularity	.25	.19	−.25	.21
Normal Vote	.24	.25	.18	.27
State Partisanship	8.38	22.08	−.75	20.94
State Change in PCDI	−.78	1.48	.21	1.48
Constant	28.52*	11.63	30.53*	12.80
R^2 Full Purging Equation	.39		.53	
R^2 Just Exogenous Variables	.11		.33	
R^2 Instrument Regressed on Exogenous Variables	.28		.63	

@$p < .10$ *$p < .05$ **$p < .01$
Note: N = 49.

Notes

1. We have a supplementary table that lists another 199 papers that were examined for this analysis, along with a brief explanation as to why they were not included in this review. This supplementary table and a comprehensive bibliography of articles on negative advertising are available for examination or download at http://fas-polisci.rutgers.edu/~lau/.

2. We also recorded a wide array of information about each study, including the disciplinary affiliations of the researchers; the nature of the subjects (students, general public) and of the advertisements (video and audio, written text); the substantive focus of an advertisement (issue or image); whether the content of the negative ads was directly coded or manipulated by the researcher or inferred from secondary sources; the office being contested; whether actual candidates

were used in the advertisement; the gender, race, and incumbency status of each candidate; and so on. In theory, each of these variables could be used as a moderator variable in the meta-analysis, although in practice the number of findings was too small for us to consider more than a few of them; and, more important, our primary goal was a bottom-line assessment of the effects of negative ads. We consider these additional variables after presenting the main results.

3. The formula for d becomes less straightforward in research involving factorial designs, but it is algebraically equivalent. These formulas can be found in the standard sources on meta-analysis cited previously.

4. For example, only significance levels were reported in some studies. In such instances, we adopted the following conventions. If the p value was reported as $< .01$, we assumed that $t = 2.75$; if the reported p was $< .05$, we assumed that $t = 2.25$; if the effect was not significant but sufficient information was provided to determine its direction, we assumed that $t = 1.0$; and if the effect was not significant and no indication was given of the direction of the effect, we assumed that $t = 0$. These approximations assumed sample sizes of 100, in which case the t distribution closely approximates the normal distribution. For smaller sample sizes we adjusted the presumed t value upward.

5. This discussion is based on the presentation by Hunter and Schmidt (1990), who provide numerous examples and describe a wide range of possible adjustments to individual effect sizes.

6. In such cases, the effect sizes we calculated compare the positive ad condition with the negative ad condition.

7. A few studies contrast negative ads with a "no advertisement" control condition. These studies were also assumed to involve a "half-strength" treatment.

8. Very few of the nonexperimental studies present any estimates of the number of positive or negative ads to which a typical survey respondent was exposed. For these studies we somewhat arbitrarily set the level at two. Our conclusions do not change if this level is set at either one or three.

9. We do not mean to impugn the value of more descriptive accounts of individual campaigns; we have read, enjoyed, and learned from many of these ourselves (see, for example, Pomper et al. 2001). Their purpose is simply different from ours here.

10. The special elections due to resignations include California, 1992, after Pete Wilson resigned to serve as the state's governor; Oklahoma, 1994, after David Boren resigned to become president of the University of Oklahoma; Tennessee, 1994, after Al Gore resigned to serve as vice president in the Clinton administration; Oregon, 1995, after Bob Packwood was forced to resign by the Senate's Ethics Committee; and Kansas, 1996, during the regular election cycle, after Bob Dole resigned to run as the Republican nominee for president. Those due to deaths include North Dakota, 1992, to replace Quentin Burdick; Georgia, 2000, to replace Paul Coverdell; and Missouri, 2002, to replace Mel Carnahan.

11. An earlier reader of this manuscript commented that by searching for sto-

ries that contained the names of *both* candidates, we were biasing our sample to disproportionately include those in which the two candidates were criticizing each other. A story about a speech by one of the candidates announcing a new policy, say, where the opponent's position is never mentioned, would not show up in our sample. In practice, such fears are misplaced. Journalistic norms dictate that any story about a candidate in an upcoming election must at least mention the office this candidate is running for and who the opponent is. Searching for articles containing the names of both major-party candidates was simply a practical solution to the problem of locating relevant articles. Particularly when the candidates have fairly common names, searching for articles with only one or the other candidate's name (but not both) simply identifies far too many articles that have nothing to do with the Senate campaign.

We used Lexis/Nexis as our primary database, turning to Dow Jones only when we could not find sufficient articles from Lexis/Nexis. We made this choice for two reasons. First, we found the user interface of Lexis/Nexis easier to use, no small advantage when multiplied over 6,000 articles. Second, although there is a good deal of overlap between the two, Lexis/Nexis included (at least it did when we were collecting articles; the holdings of these two databases are regularly changing) a somewhat larger proportion of the five largest newspapers in each state, another nontrivial advantage.

12. Democrat Pat Leahy faced a local celebrity, "Farmer Fred" Tuttle, who had been featured in a recent PBS documentary about a Vermont farmer running for Congress. Tuttle got into the Senate election only to oppose the rich carpetbagging Boston lawyer who had moved to Vermont to run against Leahy, and Tuttle upset him in the Republican primary, 55 percent to 45 percent. Tuttle started the campaign by saying he liked Senator Leahy, who he believed had been doing a good job. He drove around in a pickup truck with a "Leahy for Senate" bumper sticker, and his own wife said he was not qualified to be a senator. The two candidates spent most of the campaign praising each other, and Leahy easily won the November election, 72 percent to 22 percent. Of course, Tuttle's chances were not helped when he had to go back on his one campaign pledge, which was not to spend more than $100 on the campaign. He held a dollar-a-plate fund-raising picnic on his farm, and so many people bought tickets that he had to rent several port-o-johns, which shot his campaign budget.

13. We can also partially establish the validity of our data by comparing it to somewhat grosser categorizations of the Senate campaigns. In the appendix to their seminal article, Ansolabehere et al. (1994) report a coding of the 1992 Senate campaigns by two political consultants into three categories of "mostly positive," "mixed," and "mostly negative." We conducted an ANOVA using their categorization as the independent variable and our measure of campaign tone as the dependent variable. Again, our data are highly consistent with theirs: We find a mean of 40 percent negative campaigning in the states they categorized as having "mostly negative" campaigns, with a mean of 29.7 percent in their "mixed" states and a mean of just 27 percent negative campaigning in their "mostly positive" states, $F(1,31) = 7.30$, $p < .01$ for the linear trend.

14. Most statistical procedures assume that all cases are randomly selected from some larger pool and are thus independent of each other. Such assumptions would not hold if the same individuals appeared more than once in the data, as is the case in this data set. The saving grace for us is that the unit of analysis is not so much the candidate as the candidate–opponent pairing, and that pairing is always unique.

15. It is conventional to rely on measures of state-level partisanship developed by Wright, Erikson, and McIver (1985). Their data come from surveys conducted between 1974 and 1982, at best six years before any of the elections considered here. We updated the Wright, Erikson, and McIver data by creating our own cumulative data set from all ANES surveys conducted between 1988 and 1996 (including the Senate election study). This cumulative data set contained on average more than 500 cases per state, with the actual samples varying between a low of 153 for Hawaii to a high of 1,847 for California. We then created "updated" partisanship figures for each state by averaging our figures from 1988 to 1996 with Wright et al. data from 1974 to 1982. Our new state partisanship data correlate .92 with the original data presented by Wright et al.

16. We employ data originally coded by Alan Gerber (1998), who was kind enough to share his data for the 1992 elections with us. The authors coded the data from the remaining election years. All of these data are available from our website.

17. Indeed, we created a measure of the *projected* outcome of the race, and this measure correlates –.63 with our simple measure of relative campaign negativism. Clearly, candidates who expect to lose disproportionately go negative (see chapter 3 for more details).

18. The *National Journal* publishes these data in the issue a week or two before each election—or did, until 1998. We are particularly indebted to Jerry Hagstrom, who gathered these data for the *Journal* over the past two decades and shared his 1998 data with us, even though it ultimately was not published in the magazine. We created dummy variables for all polling firms and all media consultants who, during the 1988 to 1998 period, worked for at least three different candidates in at least three different states. These last dummy variables are designed to capture the differential proclivities of the various campaign consultants to recommend going negative in seemingly similar situations across elections. These data, along with our measures of campaign tone and candidate quality, are available from our website at http://fas-polisci.rutgers.edu/~lau/.

REFERENCES

*Items included in the meta-analysis in chapter 2.

Abramowitz, Alan I. 1988. "Explaining Senate Election Outcomes." *American Political Science Review* 82 (June): 385–404

Abramowitz, Alan I., and Jeffrey A. Segal. 1992. *Senate Elections.* Ann Arbor: University of Michigan Press.

Achen, Christopher H., and W. Phillips Shively. 1995. *Cross-Level Inference.* Chicago: University of Chicago Press.

Aldrich, John H. 1995. *Why Parties? The Origin and Transformation of Party Politics in America.* Chicago: University of Chicago Press.

Anez, Bob. 2002. "Senate Race Turns into One of Oddest in State History," Associated Press State and Local Wire (October 23).

*Ansolabehere, Stephen, and Shanto Iyengar. 1995. *Going Negative: How Political Advertisements Shrink and Polarize the Electorate.* New York: Free Press.

Ansolabehere, Stephen, Shanto Iyengar, Adam Simon, and Nicholas Valentino. 1994. "Does Attack Advertising Demobilize the Electorate?" *American Political Science Review* 88 (December): 829–838.

Aucoin, Don, and Frank Phillips. 1996. "Last Round," *Boston Globe* (October 29), A1.

*Babbitt, Paul R., and Richard R. Lau. 1994. "The Impact of Negative Political Campaigns on Political Knowledge." Paper delivered at the annual meeting of the Southern Political Science Association, Atlanta.

Barone, Michael, Richard Cohen, and Grant Ujifusa. 2003. *The Almanac of American Politics 2004.* Washington, D.C.: National Journal.

Barone, Michael, and Grant Ujifusa. 1999. *The Almanac of American Politics 2000.* Washington, D.C.: National Journal.

Barry, Thomas E. 1993. "Comparative Advertising: What Have We Learned in Two Decades?" *Journal of Advertising Research* 33 (March/April): 19–29.

Bartels, Larry M. 1991. "Instrumental and 'Quasi-Instrumental' Variables." *American Journal of Political Science* 35 (August): 777–800.

———. 1993. "Messages Received: The Political Impact of Media Exposure." *American Political Science Review* 87 (June): 267–285.

———. 1996. Review of *Going Negative* by Stephen Ansolabehere and Shanto Iyengar. *Public Opinion Quarterly* 60 (3): 456–461.

Bartels, Larry M., et al. 1998. *Campaign Reform: Insights and Evidence.* Report of the Task Force on Campaign Reform, funded by the Pew Charitable Trusts. The Woodrow Wilson School of Public and International Affairs, Princeton University.

Bartels, Larry M., and Lynn Vavreck. 2000. *Campaign Reform: Insights and Evidence.* Ann Arbor: University of Michigan Press.

*Basil, Michael, Caroline Schooler, and Byron Reeves. 1991. "Positive and Negative Political Advertising: Effectiveness of Ads and Perceptions of Candidates." In Frank Biocca (Ed.), *Television and Political Advertising,* Vol. 1, 245–261. Hillsdale, N.J.: Lawrence Erlbaum.

Becker, Betsy Jane. 1994. "Combining Significance Levels." In Harris Cooper and Larry V. Hedges (Eds.), *The Handbook of Research Synthesis.* New York: Russell Sage Foundation.

Begg, Colin B. 1994. "Publication Bias." In Harris Cooper and Larry V. Hedges (Eds.), *The Handbook of Research Synthesis.* New York: Russell Sage Foundation.

Berelson, Bernard R., Paul F. Lazarsfeld, and William N. McPhee. 1954. *Voting.* Chicago: University of Chicago Press.

Brack, Reginald K., Jr. 1994. "How to Clean Up Gutter Politics." *New York Times* (December 27), A21.

Brians, Craig L., and Martin P. Wattenberg. 1996. "Campaign Issue Knowledge and Salience: Comparing Reception from TV Commercials, TV News, and Newspapers." *American Journal of Political Science* 40 (January): 172–193.

Bryce, James Lord. [1888]. 1995. *The American Commonwealth.* Indianapolis: Liberty Fund.

Budesheim, Thomas L., David A. Houston, and Stephen J. DePaola. 1996. "Persuasiveness of In-Group and Out-Group Political Messages: The Case of Negative Political Campaigning." *Journal of Personality and Social Psychology* 70 (March): 523–534.

*Bullock, David A. 1994. The Influence of Political Attack Advertising on Undecided Voters: An Experimental Study of Campaign Message Strategy. Unpublished Ph.D. Dissertation, University of Arizona.

Burger, Timothy J. 1994. "Inhofe: Counting on 'God, Gays, and Guns,'" *Roll Call* (October 20).

Campaign Finance Institute. 2003. *Campaign Finance eGuide,* at www.cfinst .org/eguide/index.html.

Campbell, Angus. 1966. "Surge and Decline: A Study of Electoral Change." In Angus Campbell et al., *Elections and the Political Order,* chapter 2. New York: John Wiley.

Campbell, James E., and Joe A. Summers. 1990. "Presidential Coattails in Senate Elections." *American Political Science Review* 84 (June): 513–524.

Canton, Don. 2000. "Sand Announces His Plan for Agriculture," *Bismarck Tribune* (September 14), 1B.

Capella, Louis, and Kathleen Hall Jamieson. 1997. *Spiral of Cynicism*. New York: Oxford.

*Capella, Louis, and Ronald D. Taylor. 1992. "An Analysis of the Effectiveness of Negative Political Campaigning." *Business and Public Affairs* (Spring): 10–17.

Carsey, Thomas M., and Gerald C. Wright. 1998. "State and National Factors in Gubernatorial and Senatorial Elections." *American Journal of Political Science* 42 (July): 994–1002.

Colford, Steven W. 1986. "Pols Accentuated Negative." *Advertising Age* (November 10): 3, 104.

Cooper, Harris, and Larry V. Hedges, eds. 1994. *The Handbook of Research Synthesis*. New York: Russell Sage Foundation.

Cunningham, Noble E., Jr. 1972. "Election of 1800." In Arthur M. Schlesinger Jr. (Ed.), *The Coming to Power*. New York: McGraw-Hill.

Dewar, Helen. 2003. "Next Year's Senate Races Giving Both Parties Reason to Worry," *Washington Post* (September 15), A09.

Dimock, Michael A., and Gary C. Jacobson. 1995. "Checks and Choices: The House Bank Scandal's Impact on Voters in 1992." *Journal of Politics* 57 (November): 1143–1159.

Downing, Kimberly A. 1996. Debating Politics: The 1992 Presidential Debates, Media Interpretation, and Implications for Public Judgment. Ph.D. Dissertation, Rutgers University.

Downs, Anthony. 1957. *An Economic Theory of Democracy*. New York: Harper.

Estrich, Susan. 1993. "Mudslinging Is Big Voter Turnoff," *USA Today* (June 10), 11A.

Fenno, Richard F., Jr. 1996. *Senators on the Campaign Trail: The Politics of Representation*. Norman: University of Oklahoma Press.

*Finkel, Steven E., and John Geer. 1998. "A Spot Check: Casting Doubt on the Demobilizing Effect of Attack Advertising." *American Journal of Political Science* 42 (April): 573–595.

Fisher, R. A. 1932. *Statistical Methods for Research Workers*. 4th ed. London: Oliver & Boyd.

Fiske, Susan T., and Shelley E. Taylor. 1991. *Social Cognition*. New York: McGraw-Hill.

Franklin, Charles H. 1991. "Eschewing Obfuscation? Campaigns and the Perception of U.S. Senate Incumbents." *American Political Science Review* 85 (December): 1193–1214.

———. 1992. "Candidate Influence over the Voter's Decision Calculus." Paper presented at the annual meeting of the Midwest Political Science Association, Chicago.

*Freedman, Paul, and Ken Goldstein. 1999. "Measuring Media Exposure and the Effects of Negative Campaign Ads." *American Journal of Political Science* 43: 1189–1208.

Garramone, Gina M. 1984. "Voter Responses to Negative Political Ads." *Journalism Quarterly* 61: 250–259.

————. 1985. "Effects of Negative Political Advertising: The Role of Sponsor and Rebuttal." *Journal of Broadcasting & Electronic Media* 29: 147–159.

*Garramone, Gina M., Charles T. Atkin, Bruce E. Pinkleton, and Richard T. Cole. 1990. "Effects of Negative Political Advertising on the Political Process." *Journal of Broadcasting & Electronic Media* 34 (Summer): 299–311.

Geer, John. 1998. "Campaigns, Competition, and Political Advertising." In John Geer (Ed.), *New Perspectives on Party Politics*. Baltimore: Johns Hopkins University Press.

————. 2000. "Assessing Attack Advertising: A Silver Lining." In Larry M. Bartels and Lynn Vavreck, *Campaign Reform: Insights and Evidence*, chapter 2. Ann Arbor: University of Michigan Press.

————. 2003. "Attacking Democracy: A (Partial) Defense of Negativity in Presidential Campaigns, 1960–2000." Paper presented at the annual meeting of the American Political Science Association, Philadelphia.

*Geer, John G., and Richard R. Lau. 1998. "A New Way to Model the Effects of Campaigns." Paper presented at the annual meeting of the American Political Science Association, Boston.

Gerber, Alan. 1998. "Estimating the Effect of Campaign Spending on Senate Election Outcomes Using Instrumental Variables." *American Political Science Review* 92 (June): 401–412.

Glass, Gene V., Barry McGaw, and Mary Lee Smith. 1981. *Meta-Analysis in Social Research*. Beverly Hills, Calif.: Sage.

*Goldstein, Kenneth M. 1997a. "Political Commercials in the 1996 Election." Paper prepared for delivery at the annual meeting of the Midwest Political Science Association, Chicago, April 10–12.

*————. 1997b. "Political Advertising and Political Persuasion in the 1996 Presidential Campaign." Paper prepared for delivery at the annual meeting of the American Political Science Association, Washington D.C., August 28–31.

Goldstein, Ken, and Paul Freedman. 2000. "New Evidence for New Arguments: Money and Advertising in the 1996 Senate Elections." *Journal of Politics* 62 (4): 1087–1108.

————. 2002a. "Campaign Advertising and Voter Turnout: New Evidence for a Stimulation Effect." *Journal of Politics* 64 (3): 721–740.

————. 2002b. "Lesson Learned: Campaign Advertising in the 2000 Elections." *Political Communication* 19 (1): 5–28.

Green, Donald P., and Jonathan S. Krasno. 1988. "Salvation for the Spendthrift Incumbent: Reestimating the Effects of Campaign Spending in House Elections." *American Journal of Political Science* 32 (November): 884–907.

Greenfield, Meg. 1964. "The Fine Art of President-Baiting," *The Reporter*, 31 (September 24), 29–33.

Gronbeck, Bruce E. 1994. "Negative Political Ads and American Self Images." In Arthur H. Miller and Bruce E. Gronbeck (Eds.), *Presidential Campaigns & American Self Images*. Boulder, Colo.: Westview.

Grunwald, Michael. 1996. "It's Clear: Ad Spots Tarnish Reputations," *Boston Globe* (November 3), A1.

Gunnison, Robert, and John Wildermuth. 1992. "Senate Races Turn Uglier in California," *San Francisco Chronicle* (October 27), A1.

Guskind, Robert, and J. Hagstrom. 1988. "In the Gutter," *National Journal*, 18 (November 1), 2619–2629.

*Haddock, Geoffrey, and Mark P. Zanna. 1997. "Impact of Negative Advertising on Evaluations of Political Candidates: The 1993 Canadian Federal Election." *Basic and Applied Social Psychology* 19 (June): 204–223.

Halbfinger, David W. 2004. "Under Attack, Kerry Appears to Build Momentum," *New York Times* (January 18), A22.

Hale, Jon F., Jeffrey C. Fox, and Rick Farmer. 1996. "Negative Advertisements in U.S. Senate Campaigns: The Influence of Campaign Context." *Social Science Quarterly* 77 (June): 329–343.

Hale, Scott L. 1998. "Attack Messages and Their Effects on Judgments of Political Candidates: A Random-Effects Meta-Analytic Review." Paper prepared for delivery at the annual meeting of the Midwest Political Science Association, Chicago, April 23–25.

Haskins, Jack B. 1964. "Factual Recall as a Measure of Advertising Effectiveness." *Journal of Advertising Research* 4 (January/February): 2–8.

Haynes, Audrey A., and Staci L. Rhine. 1998. "Attack Politics in Presidential Nomination Campaigns: An Examination of the Frequency and Determinants of Intermediated Negative Messages Against Opponents." *Political Research Quarterly* 31 (September): 691–721.

Henneberger, Melinda. 1994. "As Political Ads Slither into Negativity, the Real Venom Is Not Found on TV," *New York Times* (October 30), 45.

Higgins, A. Jay. 1996. "Collins, Brennan Shift into Final Gear," *Bangor Daily News* (November 1).

*Hill, Ronald P. 1989. "An Exploration of Voter Responses to Political Advertisements." *Journal of Advertising* 18 (Winter): 14–22.

*Hitchon, Jacqueline C., and Chingching Chang. 1995. "Effects of Gender Schematic Processing on the Reception of Political Commercials for Men and Women Candidates." *Communication Research* 22 (August): 430–458.

*Hitchon, Jacqueline C., Chingching Chang, and Rhonda Harris. 1997. "Should Women Emote? Perceptual Bias and Opinion Change in Response to Political Ads for Candidates of Different Genders." *Political Communication* 14 (January): 49–69.

Holbrook, Thomas M. 1996. *Do Campaigns Matter?* Thousand Oaks, Calif.: Sage.

Holtz-Bacha, Christina, Lynda Lee Kaid, and Anne Johnston. 1994. "Political Television in Western Democracies: A Comparison of Campaign Broadcasts in the United States, Germany, and France." *Political Communication* 11 (January): 67–80.

Hunter, John E., and Frank L. Schmidt. 1990. *Methods of Meta-Analysis: Correcting Error and Bias in Research Findings*. Newbury Park, Calif.: Sage.

Jackson, Robert A. 1997. "The Mobilization of U.S. State Electorates in the 1988 and 1990 Elections." *Journal of Politics* 59 (2): 520–537.

Jacobson, Gary C. 1978. "The Effects of Campaign Spending in Congressional Elections." *American Political Science Review* 72 (June): 469–491.

Jacobson, Gary C., and Samuel Kernell. 1983. *Strategy and Choice in Congressional Elections*, 2nd ed. New Haven, Conn: Yale University Press.

Jalonick, Mary Claire. 2002. "Senate Changes Hands Again." *CQ Weekly* 60 (November 9): 2907–2908.

Jamieson, Kathleen Hall. 1992. *Dirty Politics: Deception, Distraction, and Democracy*. New York: Oxford University Press.

Jamieson, Kathleen Hall, and Paul Waldman. 1997. "Mapping Campaign Discourse." *American Behavioral Scientist* 40 (August): 1133–1138.

———. 2000. "Watching the Adwatches." In Larry M. Bartels and Lynn Vavreck, *Campaign Reform: Insights and Evidence*, chapter 4. Ann Arbor: University of Michigan Press.

———. 2002. *The Press Effect: Politicians, Journalists, and the Stories That Shape the Political World*. New York: Oxford University Press.

Jamieson, Kathleen Hall, Paul Waldman, and Susan Sherr. 1998. "Eliminate the Negative? Defining and Refining Categories of Analysis for Political Advertisements." Paper presented at the conference on Political Advertising in Election Campaigns, Washington, D.C., April 16 and 17.

Johnson-Cartee, Karen S., and Gary A. Copeland. 1991. *Negative Political Advertising: Coming of Age*. Hillsdale, N.J.: Lawrence Erlbaum.

*Kahn, Kim Fridkin, and John G. Geer. 1994. "Creating Impressions: An Experimental Investigation of Political Advertising on Television." *Political Behavior* 16 (March): 93–116.

*Kahn, Kim Fridkin, and Patrick J. Kenney. 1998. "Negative Advertising and an Informed Electorate: How Negative Campaigning Enhances Knowledge of Senate Elections." Paper presented to the conference on Political Advertising in Election Campaigns, Washington, D.C., April 17.

*———. 1999a. "Do Negative Campaigns Mobilize or Suppress Turnout? Clarifying the Relationship between Negativity and Participation." *American Political Science Review* 93 (4): 877–890.

———. 1999b. *The Spectacle of U.S. Senate Campaigns*. Princeton, N.J.: Princeton University Press.

Kahneman, Daniel, Paul Slovic, and Amos Tversky, eds. 1982. *Judgment under Uncertainty: Heuristics and Biases*. New York: Cambridge University Press.

*Kaid, Lynda Lee. 1997. "Effects of the Television Spots on Images of Dole and Clinton." *American Behavioral Scientist* 40 (August): 1085–1094.

*Kaid, Lynda Lee, and John Boydston. 1987. "An Experimental Study of the Effectiveness of Negative Political Advertisements." *Communication Quarterly* 35 (Spring): 193–201.

*Kaid, Lynda Lee, Mike Chanslor, and Mark Hovind. 1992. "The Influence of Program and Commercial Type on Political Advertising Effectiveness." *Journal of Broadcasting & Electronic Media* 36 (Summer): 303–320.

Kaid, Lynda Lee, and Dorothy K. Davidson. 1986. "Elements of Videostyle:

Candidate Presentation Through Television Advertising." In Lynda Lee Kaid, Dan Nimmo, and Keith R. Sanders (Eds.), *New Perspectives on Political Advertising*, 184–209. Carbondale, Ill.: Southern Illinois University Press.

Kaid, Lynda Lee, and Anne Johnston. 1991. "Negative Versus Positive Television Advertising in U.S. Presidential Campaigns, 1960–1988." *Journal of Communication* 41: 53–64.

*Kaid, Lynda Lee, Chris M. Leland, and Susan Whitney. 1992. "The Impact of Televised Political Ads: Evoking Viewer Responses in the 1988 Presidential Campaign." *Southern Speech Communication Journal* 57 (Summer): 285–295.

Kaid, Lynda Lee, John C. Tedesco, and Lori Melton McKinnon. 1996. "Presidential Ads as Nightly News: A Content Analysis of 1988 and 1992 Televised Adwatches." *Journal of Broadcasting & Electronic Media* 40 (Summer): 297–308.

Kanetkar, Vinay, Martin G. Evans, Shirley Anne Everell, Diane Irvine, and Zeeva Millman. 1995. "The Effect of Scale Changes on Meta-Analysis of Multiplicative and Main Effects Models." *Educational and Psychological Measurement* 55 (April): 206–224.

Kanouse, David E., and L. Reid Hanson. 1972. "Negativity in Evaluation." In Edward E. Jones et al. (Eds.), *Attribution: Perceiving the Causes of Behavior*. Morristown, N.J.: General Learning Press.

Karrh, James A., and David H. Halpern. 1997. "Nothing to Lose? Assessing the Impact of Competitive Position on Responses to Negative Political Advertising." Paper prepared for delivery at the annual conference of the American Academy of Advertising, St. Louis.

Kelley, Stanley, Jr. 1960. *Political Campaigning: Problems in Creating an Informed Electorate*. Washington: Brookings.

Key, V.O., and Milton C. Cummings, Jr. 1966. *The Responsible Electorate: Rationality in Presidential Voting, 1936–1960*. Cambridge, Mass.: Harvard University Press.

*King, Erika G., Robert W. Hendersen, and Hong C. Chen. 1998. "Viewer Response to Positive vs. Negative Ads in the 1996 Presidential Campaign." Paper prepared for delivery at the annual meeting of the Midwest Political Science Association, Chicago, April 23–25.

Kocieniewski, David. 2002. "Forrester on Defensive for Old Newspaper Columns," *New York Times* (October 15), B1.

Krasno, Jonathan S. 1994. *Challengers, Competition, and Reelection*. New Haven: Yale University Press.

Laczniak, Gene R., and Clarke L. Caywood. 1987. "The Case For and Against Televised Political Advertising: Implications for Research and Public Policy." *Journal of Public Policy and Marketing* 6 (Spring): 16–32.

*Lang, Annie. 1991. "Emotion, Formal Features, and Memory for Televised Political Advertisements." In Frank Biocca (Ed.), *Television and Political Advertising*, Vol. 1, 221–244. Hillsdale, N.J.: Lawrence Erlbaum.

Lau, Richard R. 1982. "Negativity in Political Perception." *Political Behavior* 4 (December): 353–378.

———. 1985. "Two Explanations for Negativity Effects in Political Behavior." *American Journal of Political Science* 29 (February): 119–138.

Lau, Richard R., and Gerald M. Pomper. 2001a. "Effects of Negative Campaigning on Turnout in U.S. Senate Elections, 1988–1998." *Journal of Politics* 63 (August): 804–819.

———. 2001b. "Negative Campaigning by U.S. Senate Candidates." *Party Politics* 7 (January): 69–87.

———. 2002. "Effectiveness of Negative Campaigning in U.S. Senate Elections." *American Journal of Political Science* 46 (January): 47–66.

*Lau, Richard R., Gerald Pomper, and Grace A. Mumoli. 1998. "Effects of Negative Campaigning on Senate Election Outcomes: 1988, 1990, 1994, & 1996." Paper prepared for delivery at the annual meeting of the Midwest Political Science Association, Chicago, April 23–26.

Lau, Richard R., and David P. Redlawsk. 1997. "Voting Correctly." *American Political Science Review* 91 (September): 585–598.

Lau, Richard R., Lee Sigelman, Caroline Heldman, and Paul Babbitt. 1999. "The Effects of Negative Political Advertisements: A Meta-Analytic Assessment." *American Political Science Review* 93 (December): 851–875.

Lazarsfeld, Paul F., Bernard R. Berelson, and Hazel Gaudet. 1948. *The People's Choice*. New York: Columbia University Press.

League of Women Voters of Los Angeles. 2003. Campaign Watch Commission, at www.lwvlosangeles.org/CampaignWatch.html.

*Lemert, James B., William R. Elliot, James M. Bernstein, William L. Rosenberg, and Karl J. Nestvold. 1991. *News Verdicts, the Debates, and Presidential Campaigns*. New York: Praeger.

Lewis-Beck, Michael, and Tom Rice. 1992. *Forecasting Elections*. Washington: CQ Press.

Lichter, S. Robert, and Richard E. Noyes. 1996. *Good Intentions Make Bad News*. Lanham, Md.: Rowman & Littlefield.

Lin, Yang. 1996. "Empirical Studies of Negative Political Advertising: A Quantitative Review Using a Method of Combined Citation and Content Analysis." *Scientometrics* 37 (September): 385–399.

*Luskin, Robert C., and Christopher Bratcher. 1994. "Negative Campaigning, Partisanship, and Turnout." Paper prepared for delivery at the annual meeting of the Midwest Political Science Association, New York.

Madison, James. 1941. *The Federalist*, No. 51 [1787]. New York: Modern Library.

Mann, Thomas E., and Norman J. Ornstein, eds. 1983. *The American Elections of 1982*. Washington, D.C.: American Enterprise Institute for Public Policy Research.

*Martinez, Michael D., and Tad Delegal. 1990. "The Irrelevance of Negative Campaigns to Political Trust: Experimental and Survey Results." *Political Communication and Persuasion* 7 (January/ March): 25–40.

*Mathews, Douglas, and Beth Dietz-Uhler. 1998. "The Black-Sheep Effect: How Positive and Negative Advertisements Affect Voters' Perceptions of the Sponsor of the Advertisement." *Journal of Applied Social Psychology* 28 (October 16): 1903–1915.

Mayer, William G. 1996. "In Defense of Negative Campaigning." *Political Science Quarterly* 111 (Fall): 437–455.

*McBride, Allan, Robert Toburen, and Dan Thomas. 1993. "Does Negative Campaign Advertising Depress Voter Turnout? Evidence from Two Election Campaigns." Unpublished manuscript.

McCombs, Maxwell E., and Donald L. Shaw. 1972. "The Agenda-Setting Function of the Mass Media." *Public Opinion Quarterly* 36 (Summer): 176–187.

McConnell v. FEC. 2003. U.S. Supreme Court, No. 02–1674 (December 10).

Melton, R. H., and Richard Morin. 2000. "Robb Pulls Even With Allen in Poll," *Washington Post* (October 29), A01.

*Merritt, Sharyne. 1984. "Negative Political Advertising: Some Empirical Findings." *Journal of Advertising* 13 (Fall): 27–38.

Mittal, Banwari. 1994. "Public Assessment of TV Advertising: Faint Praise and Harsh Criticism." *Journal of Advertising Research* 34 (January/February): 35–53.

Morrison, Jane Ann. 1998. "Voters Tuned In, Turned Off by TV ads," *Las Vegas Review-Journal* (November 9), 1B.

Mosteller, Fred, and R. R. Bush. 1954. "Selected Quantitative Techniques." In Gardner Lindzey (Ed.), *Handbook of Social Psychology*, Vol. 1. Cambridge, Mass.: Addison-Wesley.

Muehling, Darrel D., Jeffrey J. Stoltman, and Sanford Grossbart. 1990. "The Impact of Comparative Advertising on Levels of Message Involvement." *Journal of Advertising* 19 (Winter): 41–50.

*Newhagen, John E., and Byron Reeves. 1991. "Emotion and Memory Responses for Negative Political Advertising: A Study of Television Commercials Used in the 1988 Presidential Election." In Frank Biocca (Ed.), *Television and Political Advertising*, Vol. 1, 197–220. Hillsdale, N.J.: Lawrence Erlbaum.

Nowell, Paul. 1996. "Gantt Vows Response to Helms TV Ad about Race, Affirmative Action," *Durham Herald-Sun* (October 24), A1.

Nyhan, David. 1996. "An Artful Debate, and a Clear Choice," *Boston Globe* (October 30), A17.

Orwin, Robert G. 1983. "A Fail-Safe *N* for Effect Size." *Journal of Educational Statistics* 8 (Summer): 157–159.

Patterson, Thomas E. 1994. *Out of Order.* New York: Vintage.

Perloff, Richard M., and Dennis Kinsey. 1992. "Political Advertising as Seen by Consultants and Journalists." *Journal of Advertising Research* 32: 53–60.

Pfau, Michael, and Henry C. Kenski. 1990. *Attack Politics: Strategy and Defense.* New York: Praeger.

*Pfau, Michael, Henry C. Kenski, Michael Nitz, and John Sorenson. 1989. "Use of the Attack Message Strategy in Political Campaign Communication." Paper prepared for delivery at the annual meeting of the Speech Communication Association, San Francisco.

Phillips, Joseph M., and Ernest P. Goss. 1995. "The Effect of State and Local Taxes on Economic Development: A Meta-Analysis." *Southern Economic Journal* 62 (October): 320–333.

*Pinkleton, Bruce E. 1997. "The Effects of Negative Comparative Political Advertising on Candidate Evaluations and Advertising Evaluations: An Exploration." *Journal of Advertising* 26 (Spring): 19–29.

*———. 1998. "Effects of Print Comparative Political Advertising on Political Decision-Making and Participation." *Journal of Communication* 48 (Autumn): 24–36.

*Pinkleton, Bruce E., and Gina M. Garramone. 1992. "A Survey of Responses to Negative Political Advertising: Voter Cognition, Affect, and Behavior." Proceedings of the 1992 Conference of the American Academy of Advertising, 127–133.

Plato. 1945. *The Republic.* Edited by Francis Cornford. New York: Oxford University Press.

Pomper, Gerald M., et al. 2001. *The Election of 2000.* New York: Chatham House.

Pomper, Gerald M., and Ingrid W. Reed. 1999. "New Jersey Congressional Campaigns in 1998: 'Not Bad but Not Enough.'" New Brunswick, N.J.: Eagleton Institute of Politics.

Potter, Trevor, and Kirk L. Jowers. 2002. "Summary Analysis of Bipartisan Campaign Finance Reform Act," Brookings Institution, at www.brook.edu/gs/cf/headlines/finalapproval.htm.

Procter, David E., William J. Schenck-Hamlin, and Karen A. Haase. 1994. "Exploring the Role of Gender in the Development of Negative Political Advertisements." *Women & Politics* 14: 1–22.

Purdum, Todd S. 1998. "Money Politics Wasn't Defeated in California," *New York Times* (June 7): 1, 4.

Putrevu, Sanjay, and Kenneth R. Lord. 1994. "Comparative and Noncomparative Advertising: Attitudinal Effects under Cognitive and Affective Involvement Conditions." *Journal of Advertising* 23 (June): 77–91.

*Rahn, Wendy M., and Rebecca Hirshorn. 1995. "Political Advertising and Public Mood: An Experimental Study of Children's Political Orientations." Paper prepared for presentation at the annual meeting of the American Political Science Association, Chicago.

———. 1999. "Political Advertising and Public Mood: A Study of Children's Political Orientations." *Political Communication* 16 (October): 387–407.

Raju, Nambury S., Sharon Pappas, and Charmon Parker Williams. 1989. "An Empirical Monte Carlo Test of the Accuracy of the Correlation, Covariance, and Regression Slope Models for Assessing Validity Generalization." *Journal of Applied Psychology* 74 (December): 901–911.

Riker, William H. 1996. *The Strategy of Rhetoric: Campaigning for the American Constitution.* New Haven: Yale University Press.

*Roberts, Marilyn S. 1995. "Political Advertising: Strategies for Influence." In Kathleen E. Kendall (Ed.), *Presidential Campaign Discourse: Strategic Communication Problems,* 179–99. Albany: SUNY Press.

Roberts, Reginald, and R. Michael Alvarez. 1996. "Campaign Advertising and Campaign Strategy." Unpublished manuscript, California Institute of Technology.

*Roddy, Brian L., and Gina M. Garramone. 1988. "Appeals and Strategies of Negative Political Advertising." *Journal of Broadcasting & Electronic Media* 32 (Fall): 415–427.

Roese, Neal J., and Gerald N. Sande. 1993. "Backlash Effects in Attack Politics." *Journal of Applied Social Psychology* 23 (August): 632–653.

Rogers, John C., and Terrell G. Williams. 1989. "Comparative Advertising Effectiveness: Practitioners' Perceptions versus Academic Research Findings." *Journal of Advertising Research* 29 (October/November): 22–36.

Romer, Thomas, and James Snyder. 1994. "An Empirical Investigation of the Dynamics of PAC Contributions." *American Journal of Political Science* 38 (August): 745–769.

Rosenstone, Steven. 1983. *Forecasting Presidential Elections.* New Haven: Yale University Press.

Rosenthal, Robert. 1979. "The 'File Drawer' Problem and Tolerance for Null Results." *Psychological Bulletin* 86 (May): 638–641.

Sabato, Larry J. 1993. *Feeding Frenzy: How Attack Journalism Has Transformed American Politics.* New York: Free Press.

Sack, Kevin. 1998. "From Sea to Shining Sea, the TV Campaign Is All Attack Ads, All the Time," *New York Times* (30 October 1998), A30.

Salmore, Barbara G., and Stephen A. Salmore. 1989. *Candidates, Parties and Campaigns,* 2nd ed. Washington: CQ Press.

*Schultz, Cindy, and S. Mark Pancer. 1997. "Character Attacks and Their Effects on Perceptions of Male and Female Political Candidates." *Political Psychology* 18 (March): 93–102.

*Shapiro, Michael A., and Robert H. Rieger. 1992. "Comparing Positive and Negative Political Advertising on Radio." *Journalism Quarterly* 69 (Spring): 135–145.

Shaw, Daron R. 1999. "The Effects of TV Ads and Candidate Appearances on Statewide Presidential Votes, 1988–1996." *American Political Science Review* 93 (June): 345–362.

Siegel, Joel. 2000. "Fierce Slapfest in New TV Ads," *New York Daily News* (October 26), 4.

Simon, Adam. 2002. *The Winning Message: Candidate Behavior, Campaign Discourse, and Democracy.* Cambridge: Cambridge University Press.

Skaperdas, Stergios, and Bernard Grofman. 1995. "Modeling Negative Campaigning." *American Political Science Review* 89 (March): 49–61.

Squire, Peverill. 1989. "Challengers in U.S. Senate Elections." *Legislative Studies Quarterly* 14: 531–548.

———. 1992. "Challenger Quality and Voting Behavior in U.S. Senate Elections." *Legislative Studies Quarterly* 17 (May): 247–263.

Stanley, T. D., and Stephen B. Jarrell. 1989. "Meta-Regression Analysis: A Quantitative Method of Literature Surveys." *Journal of Economic Surveys* 3 (April): 161–170.

*Sulfaro, Valerie A. 1998. "Political Sophistication and the Presidential Campaign: Citizen Reactions to Campaign Advertisements." Paper prepared for delivery at the annual meeting of the Midwest Political Science Association, Chicago, April 23–25.

Texas Ethics Commission. 2003. Code of Fair Campaign Practices, at www-.ethics.state.tx.us/forms/cfcp.pdf.

Theilmann, John, and Allen Wilhite. 1998. "Campaign Tactics and the Decision to Attack." *Journal of Politics* 60 (November): 1050–1062.

*Thorson, Esther, William G. Christ, and Clarke Caywood. 1991. "Selling Candidates Like Tubes of Toothpaste: Is the Comparison Apt?" In Frank Biocca (Ed.), *Television and Political Advertising*, Vol. 1, 145–172. Hillsdale, N.J.: Lawrence Erlbaum.

*Thorson, Esther, Ekaterina Ognianova, James Coyle, and Frank Denton. 1996. "Negative Political Ads and Negative Citizen Orientations Toward Politics." Unpublished manuscript.

Timmerman, Luke. 1998. "Early Turnout High in County," *Capital Times* (Madison, Wisconsin; November 3), 1A.

Timpone, Richard J. 1998. "Structure, Behavior, and Voter Turnout in the United States. *American Political Science Review* 92 (March): 145–158.

*Tinkham, Spencer F., and Ruth Ann Weaver-Lariscy. 1991. "Advertising Message Strategy in U.S. Congressional Campaigns: Its Impact on Election Outcome." *Current Issues and Research in Advertising* 13 (Spring/Summer): 207–226.

*———. 1993. "A Diagnostic Approach to Assessing the Impact of Negative Political Television Commercials." *Journal of Broadcasting & Electronic Media* 37 (Fall): 377–400.

*———. 1994. "Ethical Judgments of Political Television Commercials as Predictors of Attitude Toward the Ad." *Journal of Advertising* 23 (September): 43–57.

———. 1995. "Incumbency and Its Perceived Advantage: A Comparison of 1982 and 1990 Congressional Advertising Strategies." *Political Communication* 12 (July): 291–304.

Trent, Judith S., and Teresa Chandler Sabourin. 1993. "When the Candidate Is a Woman: The Content and Form of Televised Negative Advertising." In Cynthia Berryman-Fink, Deborah Ballard-Reisch, and Lisa H. Newman (Eds.), *Communication and Sex Role Socialization*, 233–268. New York: Garland.

*Wadsworth, Anne Johnston, Philip Patterson, Lynda Lee Kaid, Ginger Cullers, Drew Malcomb, and Linda Lamirand. 1987. " 'Masculine' vs. 'Feminine' Strategies in Political Ads: Implications for Female Candidates." *Journal of Applied Communication* 15 (Spring/Fall): 77–94.

*Wattenberg, Martin P., and Craig L. Brians. 1999. "Negative Campaign Advertising: Demobilizer or Mobilizer?" *American Political Science Review* 93 (December): 891–899.

*Weaver-Lariscy, Ruth Ann, and Spencer F. Tinkham. 1996. "Advertising Message Strategies in U.S. Congressional Campaigns: 1982, 1990." *Journal of Current Issues and Research in Advertising* 18 (Spring): 53–66.

*Weigold, Michael F. 1992. "Negative Political Advertising: Individual Differences in Responses to Issue vs. Image Ads." Proceedings of the 1992 Conference of the American Academy of Advertising.

Welch, Susan, and John R. Hibbing. 1997. "The Effects of Charges of Corruption on Voting Behavior in Congressional Elections, 1982–1990." *Journal of Politics* 59 (February): 226–239.

West, Darrell M. 1993. *Air Wars: Television Advertising in Election Campaigns, 1952–1992.* Washington: CQ Press.

Westyle, Mark C. 1991. *Senate Elections and Campaign Intensity.* Baltimore: Johns Hopkins University Press.

White, Halbert. 1980. "Heteroskedasticity-Consistent Covariance Matrix Estimator and a Direct Test for Heteroskedasticity." *Econometrica* 48 (4): 817–838.

Will, George F. 1994. "Fingernails across the Blackboard," *Newsweek* (October 31), 72.

Wirthlin, Richard. 1987. "Negative Spots Likely to Return in Election '88." *Advertising Age* (September 14): 3, 70–78.

Wright, Gerald C., Robert S. Erikson, and John P. McIver. 1985. "Measuring State Partisanship and Ideology with Survey Data." *Journal of Politics* 47 (May): 469–489.

INDEX

incumbents: characteristics of, as control variables, 141; effect on open-seat elections of retiring, 63, *64*, 70; factors in races involving, *44*, 45–53, *50*, 57n9; first-stage regressions for spending of, 147; margin of victory of, 62; negative campaigning effectiveness for, *44*, 46–47, 49, *50*, 51, *52*; negative campaigning involving, *30*, 33, *34*, 43–55; personal factors' influence on reelection of, *44*, 45; reelection outcomes of, 6

independent voters: negative campaigning effect on candidate choice of, 51, 53; negative campaigning effect on political efficacy perception by, 87, *88*; negative campaigning effect on turnout of, 74, 78, *79*, *84*, 84

individual-level analysis, 138

information, campaigns as disseminating, 92–93

Inhofe, James, 59–60

interactive causality, research problem of, 43

interest groups, campaign abuses by, 99

Israel, 38

issue-based negativism: effectiveness of, 48–49, 53, *54*, 91; prevalence of, *29*, 136; research coding of, *135*; substantive nature of, 93; voter turnout influenced by, 77, 84–85

Iyengar, Shanto, 9, 20, 74

Jackson, Andrew, 1

Jamieson, Kathleen Hall, 100

Jefferson, Thomas, 1

Kahn, Kim Fridkin, 29, 75, 77, 85, 136

Kelley, Stanley, Jr., 92–93, 100

Kenney, Patrick J., 29, 75, 77, 85, 136

Kerry, John F., 94–97

Kerwin, Thomas, 26

Kuwata, Kam, 41

Lau, Richard R., 42

Lazio, Rick, 25

League of Women Voters, 101–2

Lexis/Nexis news database, 134, 153

Lincoln, Abraham, 1

literature on negative campaigning, 9–22

literature review. *See* meta-analysis of research

logistic regression, 128, 129

Los Angeles, California, 101–2

Lowey, Nita, 25

Luskin, Robert C., 75

MAD, as campaign tactic, 33

Madison, James, 98, 102

Mayer, William, 94

McCombs, Maxwell E., 20

McConnell v. FEC (2003), 99

McCurdy, Dave, 59–60

media coverage: public service time for candidates, 98; of statewide races, 5; tone of, and effect on voter turnout, 75, 80; watchdog function of, 100. *See also* campaign exposure; newspapers; television

merits of negative campaigning, 92–94

meta-analysis of research, 10–11, 125–32; adjusting estimated effect sizes for, 130–32; adjusting for errors and bias in, 129–30; calculating effects for, 128–29; criteria for inclusion in, 126–27; locating studies for, 125–26; variables in, 127–28

midterm elections, as control variable, 141

Minnesota, 101

mudslinging, 75, 77–78, 85

multivariate analysis, 36

Murphy, E. F., 41

ABOUT THE AUTHORS

Richard R. Lau is a professor of political science and director of the Whitman Center for the Study of Campaigns, Elections, and Democracy at Rutgers University, where he has been since 1990. Before coming to Rutgers he taught at Carnegie Mellon University; he was also a fellow at the Center for the Study of Democratic Politics at Princeton University for the 2000–2001 academic year. In addition to studying political campaigns, Lau's interdisciplinary research focuses on information processing and voter decision making, the nature of public opinion and its links to political elites, and health psychology. He is also affiliated with the Institute of Health, Health Care Policy, and Aging Research at Rutgers.

Gerald M. Pomper is Board of Governors Professor of Political Science (Emeritus) at Rutgers University and the Eagleton Institute of Politics. He is the author or editor of twenty books on American politics, including a quadrennial series on U.S. national elections from 1976 to 2000. He has also served as chair of the Free Speech Committee of the American Civil Liberties Union and in various local governmental positions, including president of his municipal school board. Previously holding visiting professorships abroad at Tel-Aviv, Oxford, and Australian National universities, his most recent book is *Ordinary Heroes and American Democracy*, published by Yale University Press.

Мемория через p31